Fun
Bible-Learning
Projects for
Young Teenagers

by

Stephen Parolini and Lisa Baba Lauffer

Loveland, Colorado

Dedications

This book is dedicated to all the junior highers I've ever known
(you know who you are). You taught me patience, persistence,
and how to play. Thanks.

—S.P.—

For Karl . . .

Whose love of fun and hunger for Bible learning inspire me
every day of our lives!

—L.B.L.—

Fun Bible-Learning Projects for Young Teenagers

Credits

Book Acquisitions Editor: Mike Nappa
Editor: Jane Vogel
Senior Editor/Creative Products Director: Joani Schultz
Copy Editor: Pamela Shoup
Art Director: Lisa Smith
Cover Art Director: Liz Howe
Cover Designer: Diana Walters
Cover Photographer: Craig DeMartino
Computer Graphic Artist: Randy Kady
Illustrator: Ken Bowser
Production Manager: Gingar Kunkel

Unless otherwise noted, Scriptures quoted from the Youth Bible, New Century Version,
copyright © 1991 by Word Publishing, Dallas, Texas 75039. Used by permission.

Parolini, Stephen, 1959-
    Fun Bible-learning projects for young teenagers / by Stephen Parolini and
    Lisa Baba Lauffer.
        p.   cm.
    Includes bibliographical references.
    ISBN 1-55945-796-1
    1. Bible–Children's use. 2. Bible–Study and teaching (Secondary)–Activity pro-
grams. 3. Activity programs in Christian education. I. Lauffer, Lisa Baba. II. Title.
BS618.P37 1995
268'.433–dc20   95-7800
                                                                  CIP

Printed in the United States of America.
10 9 8 7 6 5 4 3 2 1   04 03 02 01 00 99 98 97 96 95

Contents

Introduction

Caught you, didn't we? You've been flipping through books looking for new, creative junior high or middle school program ideas. You want something fun, unique, fun, easy to do, fun, easy to lead, fun...

To many young teenagers, the three most important words in life are fun, fun, and fun. But how do you give fun-loving kids the kind of spiritual food that growing Christians need?

Thought you'd never ask. You feed them a creative blend of fun and learning—like the kind infused into every idea in this book. Each project is designed to give 11- to 14-year-olds an experience they won't forget—and one that will help them understand a spiritual truth. Kids get to "do," instead of just watch or listen. And it's in the doing that kids latch onto concepts that can help them grow in faith.

It's called active learning and...wait. We could go on and on about this, but you're a junior high or middle school leader. You don't have much time for explanations—you want action (perhaps that's why you're a youth leader?). No problem. Turn the page now to find a new way of growing your kids' faith.

Really. That's it. That's the introduction. Now get out there and have some fun!

① Classroom Projects

Tonight is youth-meeting night, and you still don't have a meeting plan? Never fear, classroom projects are here! This chapter features projects with a point that require just a few easy-to-find supplies. They are perfect when you need an activity in a snap. Use them for midweek youth meetings or Sunday school classes!

TIME FOCUS: ONE HOUR.

NUMBER OF STUDENTS: UNLIMITED.

Frequent Flyer ✓

Focus of the Fun: Kids will explore the good and bad aspects of competition as they create flying machines and participate in competitions.

Supplies: Rubber bands, paper clips, stiff paper, markers, pencils, prizes for the winning pairs, masking tape, a watch with a second hand, a yardstick, and Bibles.

Form pairs and give each pair a supply of stiff paper (such as card stock or poster board) cut into squares, paper clips, rubber bands, markers, and pencils.

Say: **You have 15 minutes to create at least one "flying machine" using the items you've been given. You don't need to use all the items. When your flying machine is finished, we'll have competitions to see which machine can fly the longest distance, which can stay in the air the longest, and which can fly the straightest. You may want to create a different flying machine to compete in each of the three competitions. The winning pair in each competition will receive a prize.**

Give kids time to create their flying machines, then lead them in the following three competitions, awarding prizes to the winning pairs for each competition.

Farthest Flyer: Have kids line up behind a masking tape line at one end of a long hallway then take turns flying their flying machines down the hallway. Mark the landing location for each flying machine so you can determine a winner. You may want to give each pair two tosses. (Keep track of the longest toss by placing a marked piece of masking tape on the floor.)

Longest Flight Time: Use a watch with a second hand to determine how long each flying machine stays in the air for this competition. Give pairs each two turns to fly their flying machines. Record the times and add the two times together to determine the machine that had the longest "air time."

Straightest Flyer: Make a masking tape line straight down a long hallway (or

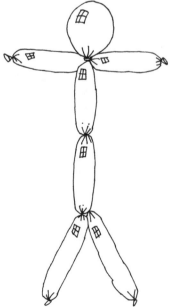

Young-Teenager Tip:
According to psychologist Helen Bee, junior highers generally think concretely but are on the brink of developing abstract thought (developing ideas and understanding the reasoning behind things). Using activities, object lessons, and projects to illustrate a point taps into young teenagers' concrete understanding and encourages them to think abstractly. *(The Developing Child* by Helen Bee)

use an existing line from a carpet or pattern on the floor). Have participants take turns flying their flying machines at least 10 feet from the starting point. Use a yardstick to determine which flying machine is closest to the straight line.

After the competitions, discuss the following questions: **What was it like creating machines that you knew would be used in competition? What were your goals as you made your flying machine? What were the good aspects of competition in this activity? in life? What were the negative aspects of competition in this activity? in life? What does this experience tell us about how we should approach competition in life?**

Have someone read aloud Philippians 3:12-14. Then discuss: **How is Paul's attitude like the way you approached this competition? How is your approach unlike Paul's attitude? How is the Christian life like a competition? What goals are important? What determines whether or not you are a winner in the Christian life? What can we learn from our flying-machine competitions that might help us better pursue the goal of a closer relationship with Christ?**

Scriptures for Deeper Study: 1 Corinthians 9:24-27; 2 Timothy 2:3-10.

Giant Challenge ✓

Focus of the Fun: Kids will make life-size Goliaths and discuss handling life's challenges.

Supplies: Bibles; 100 long, narrow balloons (the kind to make animals with—they are available at party decoration stores and balloon bouquet delivery stores); 10 tennis balls; and four old socks. (You might also want a balloon pump to make blowing up the balloons easier.)

In this project, kids will create life-size Goliaths. Because Goliath was over 9 feet tall, make sure you are in a room that has a ceiling at least 10 feet from the floor, or do this project in a parking lot or on a lawn.

Form two teams. Give each team a Bible and 50 balloons. Have teams read 1 Samuel 17.

Say: **Work as a team to make a Goliath out of the balloons I gave you. Use the Bible passage to make your Goliath the right size. When you are done, each team will have a chance to knock the other team's Goliath over, so make your Goliaths able to withstand a blow from a tennis ball.**

Give teams 30 minutes to create their Goliaths. They can twist the balloons together to form a head, arms, a torso, legs, and even Goliath's armor. Show kids how to connect balloons by carefully twisting the ends of two inflated balloons, then twisting the two balloons together at the places where they were individually twisted.

Each team will need to form a way to prop up Goliath, such as creating a tripod out of balloons that can support him in an upright fashion.

When the time is up, give each team five tennis balls and two socks. Have teams create a "sling" by tying the socks together at the toes. Then have team members try to knock down the other team's Goliath by placing a tennis ball into the sling, twirling the sling and ball above their heads, and releasing the tennis ball toward Goliath. Each team member gets one chance to knock over Goliath. The team that knocks over the other team's Goliath the most wins.

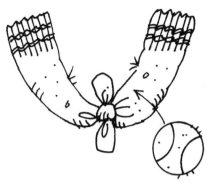

Say: **The real Goliath was not made out of balloons. What do you imagine it was like for David to face Goliath? What is one time you responded to a Goliath-like challenge the way David did? Why were you able to respond that way? What is a Goliath-like challenge you have in front of you? How can you respond to it in a David-like way?**

Scriptures for Deeper Study: 2 Samuel 22:31-43; 2 Corinthians 1:8-11; 2 Timothy 4:17-18.

Goodwill Gum

Focus of the Fun: Group members will learn how to encourage one another as they write affirming notes on gum wrappers.

Supplies: Plenty of popular "stick" gum (the kind with the paper outer wrappers), pens, tape, and Bibles.

Have kids read aloud 1 Thessalonians 5:11. Then distribute stick gum (at least five pieces to each person) along with pens and tape. (Kids can share pens and tape if necessary.)

Say: **The message of 1 Thessalonians 5:11 is that we're to uplift and encourage one another. We're going to do this by writing goodwill statements on the inside of gum wrappers. We'll place the goodwill gum in a location where any church member can take one to get a word of encouragement.**

Have kids remove the outer wrappers from the sticks of gum and work together to determine what goodwill phrases they'll write on their gum wrappers. Remind kids to write only positive statements. (You may want to look at them before kids put the wrappers back on the gum.) Kids may choose to quote a favorite Bible passage or come up with their own wise words of encouragement. For example, kids might write things such as "God loves you no matter what" or "If life's got you down, just look up... and ask God to help."

When group members have written their goodwill phrases, have volunteers share their favorites with the whole group. Then have kids tape the wrappers back onto the gum.

Have kids decorate a box to look like a large package of gum and place the goodwill gum inside. During a church service, have a member of the group explain the purpose of the goodwill gum and invite church members to take a piece of gum when they need encouragement. Have kids replenish the goodwill gum container when it gets low.

Scriptures for Deeper Study: Romans 15:1-6; 1 Corinthians 14:12.

Group Documentary

Focus of the Fun: Kids will create an impromptu documentary about themselves and grow closer to one another in the process.

Supplies: Video camera and videotape (or audiocassette recorder, blank audiocassette, and an instant-print camera), and Bibles.

For this activity, you'll need a video camera and a blank videotape. If you don't have access to a video camera, use an audiocassette recorder to record what kids say and have someone take still pictures to paste on a poster that will go with the cassette.

Have kids vote on what topic they'd most like to hear everyone talk about. For example, kids might choose a topic such as "what it means to be a friend," "my strangest family trip," "my most embarrassing moment," or "my favorite youth group memory." Encourage originality in the topics chosen, then have group members interview each other on those topics, recording the answers on videotape (or on a cassette).

Ask kids to match the tone of the answers to the tone of the question or topic. For example, a serious topic should prompt kids' honest, serious answers. But a more lively topic could have wild answers.

During the activity, take breaks to read the following Scripture passages: Mark 3:13-19; 4:35-41; 6:7-13; 8:34-35; 10:13-16; 14:27-31; and 16:14-18.

After the videotape (or cassette recording) is finished, discuss the following questions: **How are our experiences together like the faith journey the disciples took with Jesus? How are our experiences unlike the disciples' faith journey? What observations do you have about the way Jesus interacted with the disciples? about the way the disciples interacted with each other? What does our mini documentary say about our group? How are we on a faith journey similar to what the disciples were on?**

Create a running history of your group by periodically doing this activity. Combine the mini documentaries onto one tape and save that tape for kids to refer to after they've graduated into the senior high group (or beyond). This living history can be a valuable tool for helping kids see how much they've grown in Christ through the years.

Scriptures for Deeper Study: Matthew 4:18-25; 8:18-27; 13:1-17; 18:1-6; 24:1-14; 26:17-30.

Light Show

Focus of the Fun: Kids will learn the importance of each person's role as they create a light show for a favorite song about faith.

Supplies: Audiocassette player and cassettes of popular Christian music, flashlights, colored cellophane, white sheet, Bibles, and any other items the kids choose to collect.

Hang a white sheet from the ceiling near one end of your room to create a screen for the light show. Leave space behind the sheet for kids to perform.

Form groups of no more than five. Have each group choose a favorite Christian song from the tape (or tapes) you've brought. Then say: **Each group is going to create a choreographed light show for its song using the flashlights, colored cellophane, and other items. You'll set up your show behind the sheet and perform it for people sitting on the other side of the sheet to see.**

Young-Teenager Tip: The ages of 13 and 14 (around the eighth grade) are when adolescents feel most pressured to conform to their peers.

Give groups at least 20 minutes to brainstorm and practice what they'll do in their light show for their chosen song. Suggest the following ideas to get kids started.

● Flash the colored lights in sync with the rhythm of the song.
● Choose colors that represent the message of the song.
● Cast shadows of objects relating to the theme of the song.
● Choreograph and practice moving the flashlights to the music.
● Act out a scene from the song, with the lights casting the shadows of the actors onto the sheet.

After allowing time for kids to practice their light shows, dim the lights and have each group present its show to the whole group.

When the light shows are over, have someone read aloud 1 Corinthians 12:12-31. Ask: **How were your roles in these light shows like the roles we play in the body of Christ? What would happen if one of the members of your group didn't perform in the light show? What happens when we don't live out our gifts in the church? How do our gifts support and enhance one another in life as your responsibilities in the light show supported and enhanced the show?**

Scriptures for Deeper Study: Romans 12:3-8; Ephesians 4:1-6.

Machinations

Focus of the Fun: Kids will explore their individuality as they create unique machines out of everyday items.

Supplies: Bibles and any items immediately available on church grounds (everything from balloons to waste paper).

Begin this activity by reading aloud Romans 12:4-8. Then say: **Today we're going to become inventors as we live out an example of what it means to be unique creations in Christ.**

Young-Teenager Tip:
If your junior highers are frequently distracted and have a difficult time staying on task, try splitting them up into same-sex groups for activities. Sometimes, young teenagers' concern about how they'll look to the members of the opposite sex is enough to keep them from focusing on the activity at hand.

Tell kids they'll have 15 minutes to individually collect items from around the church, which they can then use to invent a machine that represents some unique trait about themselves. For example, someone might use a bunch of books to create a "reading machine" to express his or her interest in reading. Another might stack a bunch of chairs together with pots and pans from the church kitchen to create a "lazy machine" that represents his or her interest in sitting around and eating. Allow kids the freedom to be serious or funny in their creations.

After about 15 minutes, call time and have kids explain their machines' functions and what they represent about their individuality. Then have kids work together to find creative ways to connect the various machines and form one machine that represents the whole group. For example, the reading machine might sit on one of the chairs from the lazy machine.

When all the machines are connected, take a few minutes to have kids admire the final creation. Then ask: **What do these machines tell us about our group? What similarities did we discover about each other? What differences? What can we learn from this activity to help us get along better with one another?**

Scriptures for Deeper Study: 1 Corinthians 12:1-31; Jeremiah 1:4-8.

Maker of the Universe

Focus of the Fun: Kids will reflect on God's power in creating the universe as they make a room-size model of the solar system.

Supplies: Enough black construction paper (or black plastic garbage bags) to cover the ceiling of your youth room, masking tape, two beach balls, a bag of round balloons, a roll of aluminum foil, 35 old tennis balls, a roll of string, scissors, a container of pushpins, a stepladder, and three Bibles.

Say: **We are going to create a model of the solar system in this very room.** Use the following suggestions to complete this project.

● Have kids cover the ceiling with black construction paper (or black plastic garbage bags). Make sure they anchor each sheet of paper to the ceiling with many loops of masking tape, sticky side out.

● Form three groups: the Planet Group, the Moon Group, and the Star Group.

● Have the Planet Group suspend the sun and planets from the ceiling, using the following diagrams as guides. Tell the group to use the two beach balls as the sun and Jupiter and the balloons as the other planets. While some students inflate the beach balls and balloons, others can cut 2-foot pieces of string. Then they can hang the "planets" from the ceiling using tape or pushpins.

The Solar System

Sample Solar System on a Ceiling

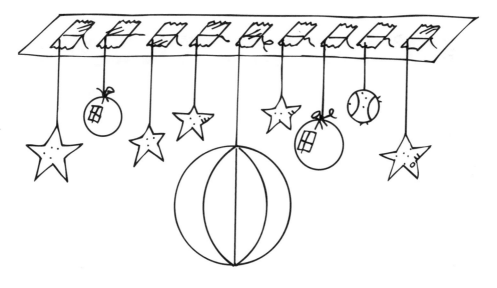

● Have the Moon Group use the tennis balls to place moons around the planets, attaching them to the ceiling in the same manner as the planets. Following is a list of the planets and the number of moons orbiting them: Earth—1, Mercury—0, Venus—0, Mars—2, Jupiter—4, Saturn—20, Uranus—5, Neptune—2, and Pluto—1.

● Tell the Star Group to cut stars out of aluminum foil and attach them to the ceiling with string in the same manner as the planets and moons. Make sure they make as many stars as students in the room (they may make more if they wish). Have this group also cut two rings out of the aluminum foil, making one ring large enough to encircle Saturn and the other large enough to encircle Uranus. Then using tape or pushpins, have them suspend the rings from the ceiling around their respective planets.

When the solar system is finished, give each group a Bible and tell groups to open their Bibles to Psalm 8. Have the Planet Group read verses 1-3 aloud, then the Moon Group read verses 4-6 aloud, and then the Star Group read verses 7-9 aloud.

Have the whole group form a circle under the "sky" and lie down with their heads toward the center of the circle to stargaze. Ask: **What do you imagine God felt as he created the universe? What thoughts go through your mind as you think about God creating our earth, all the planets, all the moons, and all the stars? What do you think about when you remember that the God who created the universe created you, too?**

Afterward, have each person take a star from the ceiling. Say: **Give your star to someone else in the room and tell that person why he or she is a star in God's creation. For example, you could say, "Stacey, you are a star because you are friendly to everyone."** Make sure each person receives a star.

Scriptures for Deeper Study: Genesis 1–2:3; Psalm 19:1-6; Isaiah 40:26; Romans 1:20.

Movie Posters

Focus of the Fun: Junior highers and middle schoolers will learn about the importance of fellowship as they create fake movie posters depicting some aspect of the group.

Supplies: Poster board, markers, film magazines (such as Premiere), and Bibles.

Form groups of no more than four and give each group a large sheet of poster board and colored markers. Explain that each group is to make a fake movie poster depicting some positive aspect of the youth group, using a format and theme similar to that of a real movie poster. (Provide magazines with actual movie ads as examples.)

For example, kids might create a poster similar to one advertising a popular adventure film that describes the "wonderful adventure of being in the youth group together." Or kids might create a poster based on a popular love story that describes the love kids have for one another. Encourage kids to be creative and to use as many ideas from the actual poster as they can in their version of the poster.

When posters are complete, have groups display them for the whole class. Then have someone read aloud 1 John 4:7-10. Discuss the following questions:

What does this passage tell us about how we should relate to one another? What aspects of this passage could be included in a definition of Christian fellowship? How is the experience of working together on these posters a small example of what it means to be in fellowship with one another? How do our posters depict fellowship? What are practical ways to grow closer together?

Scriptures for Deeper Study: John 13:34-35; 15:1-8.

Mystery Object

Focus of the Fun: Kids will illuminate "mystery objects" behind a screen to illustrate that we can have faith in God without seeing him.

Supplies: A queen-size or full-size flat sheet, a large rectangular table, masking tape, a pen, three flashlights, three Mystery Objects (for example, a table lamp, a bicycle, and a Walkman), and Bibles.

Bring all the supplies except the mystery objects to a room that can be completely darkened. If you have windows not covered by curtains, cover your windows by taping black construction paper or black plastic garbage bags to the inside. Also consider covering cracks underneath doors by placing towels on the floor along the width of the doors.

Hide the mystery objects outside the room but not too far away. You don't want the kids to see the mystery objects as they enter, but you do want to be able to get them quickly during the activity.

Bring the group into the darkened room. Say: **We're going to create a screen to hide some mystery objects.** Have your kids hang up the screen by attaching one edge of the sheet to the ceiling with the masking tape or thumbtacks. Tape the sheet 6 feet from the door, parallel to the door so the sheet hides the door. Have kids set up the table a few inches away from the sheet on the door side, with the table running the width of the screen. Then have kids use masking tape and a pen to label the flashlights #1, #2, and #3. Have kids use masking tape to tape the same numbers to the floor between the table and the door (see diagram below).

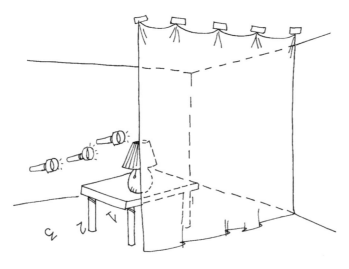

When the screen is set up, ask for three volunteers. Invite the volunteers behind the screen, give each volunteer a flashlight, and have them stand on the number corresponding to the flashlight. Then pull one object, for example the bicycle, from behind the door and place it on the table. Be as quiet as possible.

When you have the object in place, have the kids on the other side of the screen ask yes or no questions about the object. For example, kids could ask, "Does it move?" When the answer to a question is "no," another student asks a question. When the answer is "yes," one of the students with a flashlight turns his or her flashlight on (#1 goes first, #2 second, and #3 third), illuminating part of the shape of the object on the other side of the screen.

When the group guesses the object, have the flashlight holders bring the object out for the rest of the group to see. Then choose three new volunteers and repeat the process. Consider using one of the flashlight holders as an object. Have one student sit on the table, and you as the leader take his or her place with the flashlight.

When you have depleted your stock of mystery objects, gather the group for discussion. Ask: **How did you figure out what the mystery object was when you couldn't see it?** Have students read Hebrews 11:1 in unison. Ask: **How does this Scripture define faith? How do we have faith in God even though we can't see him?**

Scriptures for Deeper Study: Romans 1:20; 8:24-25; 2 Corinthians 4:18; 5:7.

Noisy Symphony

Focus of the Fun: Kids will explore what it means to praise God as they create and perform a brief symphony of praise.

Supplies: You will need to provide an audiocassette recorder, a blank audiocassette, and Bibles. In addition, kids will gather items immediately available on church grounds (including soft drink cans, light switches, squeaky shoes).

Form groups of no more than four. Have each group choose a short passage from any psalm to use as a basis for a praise symphony the whole group will perform.

Give the following instructions to the groups:

● **Your portion of the praise symphony must include a reading or singing of the Scripture passage you chose (or your paraphrase of that passage). Choose a passage that praises God for something that's meaningful to you.**

● **You must accompany the reading or singing with a musical background.**

● **The musical instruments you use for your accompaniment can be anything except a real musical instrument. You can combine items to create musical instruments. For example, you might flick a noisy light switch or use pots and pans for rhythm instruments.**

● **We'll combine the short praise parts into one continuous symphony of praise after groups have practiced their parts.**

Have groups meet in separate rooms if possible while creating their portions of the praise symphony. Then gather in the church sanctuary or another room with good acoustics to have groups perform the symphony. Determine the order groups will go in, then begin the symphony. Record the concert using a cassette recorder so kids can listen to it later. If kids are really into this activity, allow them the chance to practice the whole symphony so you can record the best possible rendition to be played for the whole church.

During the activity, discuss the following questions: **What does this activity teach us about what we need in order to praise God? How does our praise make God feel? What are ways we can praise God in everyday life?**

Scriptures for Deeper Study: Psalm 150; Luke 19:38-40.

Paper Sports

Focus of the Fun: Kids will learn how to do with fewer material things as they create implements for their favorite sport using only paper and tape.

Supplies: Large sheets of paper or newsprint, masking tape, and Bibles.

Have kids vote on their favorite sport, such as volleyball, baseball, football, basketball, or hockey. Then present kids with a supply of large paper and masking tape. Say: **Using only the paper and tape, create all the necessary equipment to play our favorite sport. When you're done making the items, we'll actually play the sport using them—so make everything as sturdy as necessary for us to enjoy the game!**

Give no further instruction, but encourage kids to work together to create the necessary items for the sport. For example, kids would need to create bases, a bat, a ball, gloves, and perhaps even hats, to play a game of baseball. Or they'd have to create a net and a volleyball for a game of volleyball.

When kids are ready, play the sport using the appropriate equipment. During the game, allow kids to stop and make adjustments to their sports equipment if necessary. The goal of the activity is for kids to create equipment that can be used more than once for the particular sport.

For fun, have kids choose a different sport each week to create equipment for and have them save the items so they can use them in the future. Take time out to discuss what kids learned in the creation of the sports implements, if appropriate.

Have a volunteer read aloud Matthew 14:15-21. Then ask: **When in everyday life must we make do with less than what we think we need? How did we overcome the lack of sports equipment to enjoy the sports anyway? What applications does this experience have for us in light of the material things we want? How can we get by with fewer material possessions in life?**

How important was it to learn from mistakes in this activity? Was playing the sport more fun than if we used actual equipment? Explain. What can we learn about working together from this activity?

Young-Teenager Tip: The one word that best describes all young teenagers is "diversity." In discussions, expect everything—from the junior higher who acts like a goofy 10-year-old to the middle schooler who speaks as clearly and thoughtfully as the wise college student. There is no "typical" young teenager.

Scriptures for Deeper Study: Matthew 17:20; Mark 12:41-44.

Pasta Builder

Focus of the Fun: Group members will explore their creative abilities as they build items out of pasta noodles and tape.

Supplies: A variety of dry pasta noodles (many shapes), tape, and Bibles.

Form groups of two or three, combining kids who don't know each other well. Place a variety of pasta on the table along with the tape (enough so all groups can use tape at the same time). Then say: **We're going to create unique sculptures using only the pasta noodles and the tape. I'm going to call out an item to build, and you're to work with your group to build that item as fast as possible. The only rule is that the finished item must be clearly recognizable as the object I call out. If any group doesn't agree that the item looks like what I've called for, we'll continue the building until another team finishes and presents the item to the group.**

Young-Teenager Tip: Junior highers and middle schoolers can get into serious discussions just as well as senior highers can—if they feel comfortable about the topic. You can avoid the giggling and the nervous laughter if you stay away from those topics that kids just don't want to talk about in a group (many groups can't talk seriously about sex, for example). When you introduce a serious topic for discussion, let your group members know up front that this is a serious discussion. That way, they'll know what behavior is expected during the discussion.

Remind kids that all group members must contribute to the creation of the various items and that they must be fair in their judgment of other groups' creations.

Call out a few items from the following list (or make up your own):
● Bicycle
● Tiger
● Chair
● House
● Telephone
● Lawn mower
● Computer
● Rabbit
● Person

(For a real challenge, have kids attempt to create depictions of emotions such as love, fear, anger, happiness, and sadness.)

Finish the activity by allowing each group time to create its own item (with as much detail as possible) for the other groups to guess. Display the finished items in your youth room for a month or so to illustrate the creative abilities of your group members.

Have volunteers read aloud Genesis 1:1–2:3. Then discuss the following questions in groups of three or four: **What was it like to create these items? How is this creative process like the way God created the world? How is it unlike Creation? What is the value of having the ability to create? Why did God give humans, but not animals, the ability to create? How does it feel to be a creative part of God's creation?**

Scriptures for Deeper Study: 2 Corinthians 5:16-21; Ecclesiastes 12:1-14.

Patterns

Focus of the Fun: Kids will create a wall hanging from patterns created by each individual, then discuss ways to encourage each other.

Supplies: Colored paper, tape, glue, markers, scissors, and Bibles.

Show kids the supplies you've provided. Say: **I want each of you to use these supplies to create a pattern that represents how you're feeling today. For example, someone might tape together a whole bunch of black pieces of paper with a few yellow streaks across them to represent feelings of sadness, but with a little bit of hope streaming through.** Encourage kids to be creative with their pattern creations and to use shapes as well as colors to express themselves.

When their patterns are complete, have kids come up to the front of the room and tape their patterns to a wall, connecting each pattern to the last to form a wall hanging consisting of all their patterns. Have group members take turns guessing what feelings each pattern represents. Then have the pattern creators explain what they intended by their patterns. Encourage kids to be sensitive to each other's feelings during this time.

Then have kids take turns reading verses from Romans 15:1-7. Have pairs discuss the following questions, then form foursomes to discuss their answers.

Ask: **What does this passage tell us about the role of encouragement in our faith lives? How does understanding each other's feelings help us know how to encourage each other? How can we be encouragers in everyday life? How does our wall hanging represent unity in our group? What can we do to build unity with each other?**

Scriptures for Deeper Study: 2 Corinthians 6:1-10; Ephesians 4:1-6.

Prayer Chains

Focus of the Fun: Kids make prayer chains to help them establish a habit of prayer.

Supplies: Three sheets of 8½×11 paper for each student, scissors, pencils, tape, a sheet of newsprint, masking tape, markers, and Bibles for students to share.

Cut each sheet of paper into 1-inch strips across the width of the paper (see diagram on page 18). You should end up with 31 strips for each student.

Say: **Today we're going to start a project that will help us pray consistently for each other over the next month.**

As a group, brainstorm a number of prayer categories, such as friends, family members, specific prayer requests in the group (for example, for someone's broken arm to heal quickly), missionaries, or teachers. List the categories on a sheet of newsprint taped to a wall.

Give each student 31 strips of paper and one pencil. On each strip, have kids write a specific prayer request from the categories on the newsprint. For example, one student might write, "That I get along better with my younger brother."

After the students have written a different prayer request on each strip (31 requests in all), have each person take one strip and make a loop out of it (with the writing on the inside), fastening it with tape. Then have each person loop a second strip through the first one and fasten it to itself with tape. Tell students to continue the process until all 31 of their strips are looped together in a chain (see diagram below). During the project, initiate a discussion about prayer requests your students have had in the past and how God answered them. Use Philippians 4:6-7 as the basis for your discussion.

When everyone has completed the project, instruct kids to take their prayer chains home. Encourage junior highers and middle schoolers to remove one link of the chain every day and pray for that request.

Scriptures for Deeper Study:
Matthew 6:6; 1 Thessalonians 5:17; 1 Timothy 2:1-4; James 5:13-16.

Rules of the Road

Focus of the Fun: Kids will make road signs that apply to Christian living.

Supplies: You'll need red, green, white, yellow, and orange construction paper. Also gather black glitter; white glitter; black, gray, yellow, and white tempera paints; four containers for holding the paint; water; four containers for holding water; paintbrushes; a roll of newsprint; masking tape; and one Bible for every four students.

If you're using powdered paints, mix them with water before your meeting.

Form groups of no more than four. Say: **We'll be creating road signs that help us travel safely down the road of our relationships with God.** Give each group one piece of construction paper. Have groups brainstorm a road sign that expresses a truth about life in Christ. Here are some ideas for road signs that groups can create:

- "Narrow Path, Straight Ahead" painted in white paint on green paper. Paint an arrow pointing up. Outline the edges of the paper with white paint.
- "DO NOT ENTER into Sin" painted in white paint on red paper. Paint the outline and outside of the circle, leaving the inside red. Paint a white line horizontally through the middle of the circle, and then paint the words above and below the white line.
- "U-TURN to Jesus" painted in black paint on white paper. Have the group paint the words and outline the edges with black paint.
- "CROSS WALK" painted in black paint on yellow paper. Before painting, turn the paper so it makes a diamond shape (with one corner at the top). Paint a cross below the words. Outline the edges in black.
- "YIELD to Christ" painted in white paint on red paper cut into a triangle. Create a white triangle in the middle and outline the words so they appear in red. Outline the edges in white paint.
- "STOP Sin" painted in white paint on red paper cut into an octagon. Outline the edges in white paint.
- "ONE WAY to God" painted in black paint on white paper. Paint an arrow pointing straight up and outline the edges in black.
- "Spirit at Work" painted in black paint on orange paper. Before painting, turn the paper so it makes a diamond shape. Outline the edges in black.
- "The world's way is a DEAD END" painted in black paint on yellow paper, turned so it makes a diamond shape. Outline the edges in black.
- "KEEP RIGHT with God" painted in black paint on white paper. Paint a median and paint an arrow going to the right of it. Outline the edges in black.

While the paint is still wet, have kids sprinkle the same color glitter on the paint (white on white and black on black) to create the reflective effect of road signs.

Then have the group collaborate to paint a road on a piece of newsprint long enough to reach from the floor to the ceiling of your youth room. Paint the road gray with a double yellow line or a dotted white line down the middle.

While the signs and road are drying, ask: **Why do we obey road signs? How do rules help us live together?** Have foursomes read Mark 12:28-31 with each student reading one verse aloud. Ask: **What do these verses say to you about God's rules for our lives? How are these rules like the road signs we made? How are these rules different from the road signs we made? What's one way you can obey the rules in this Scripture passage this week?**

When the signs and road are dry, shake the glitter onto a sheet of newsprint and return the excess to the bottle. Tape the road and signs with masking tape to one of your youth-room walls. Tape the road first, then allow each group's members to place their signs wherever they want along the road.

Scriptures for Deeper Study: Exodus 20:1-17; John 13:34; Romans 3:19-31; 7:4-12; Galatians 4:4-5.

Stick to It!

Focus of the Fun: Teams will use different methods of sticking scavenger hunt items onto paper and discuss sticking to their faith.

Supplies: A roll of masking tape, a glue stick, a bottle of white glue, a tube of Super Glue, a stapler, staples, enough 12×18-inch construction paper in assorted colors for every three students to have one piece, enough copies of the "Stick to It!" handout (p. 21) for every three kids to have one, and one Bible for every three students.

Have kids form trios. Give each trio one of the following methods of attaching items to paper: a 6-foot strip of masking tape, a glue stick, a bottle of white glue, a tube of Super Glue, or a stapler full of staples. Also give each trio a piece of construction paper and a copy of the handout.

Say: **I am giving each trio one sheet of paper, a method for sticking objects onto the paper, and the handout "Stick to It!" You have 15 minutes to go outside, find as many things from the handout as you can, and attach them to your sheet of paper.**

After 15 minutes, have the trios return inside to compare what they have collected. Then ask: **What kinds of things stuck to the paper? Why? What kinds of things wouldn't stick to the paper? Why? Which method of sticking worked best?** Wrap up the project by having trios read Romans 4:18-21 and answer the following questions: **How did Abraham stick to his faith? What do we need to stick to our faith?**

Scriptures for Deeper Study: 1 Corinthians 16:13; Colossians 1:22-23; 1 Timothy 1:18-19; 2 Timothy 1:12.

Stick to It!

1. Something red.

2. Something from nature.

3. Something that's a part of a larger object.

4. Something that reminds you of school.

5. Something that reminds you of a friend.

6. Something that makes noise.

7. Something that smells good.

8. Something edible.

9. Something blue.

10. Something green.

11. Something that feels rough.

12. Something you like.

13. Something with three colors on it.

14. Something straight.

15. Something round.

16. Something with words on it.

17. Something that used to have a different shape.

18. Something brown.

19. Something white.

20. Something made of wood.

Tubular Vision

Focus of the Fun: Kids will create binoculars to experience having different perspectives from one another.

Supplies: One Bible per student, two cardboard tubes per student (toilet paper tubes or gift wrap tubes cut into short lengths), masking tape, other bits of paper, colored plastic (such as colored plastic wrap you can find in the grocery store), scissors, straight or safety pins, a hole punch, and yarn.

Have students begin by reading 1 Peter 3:8 in unison. Ask: **What does this verse say to you about how we relate with one another? How do you put this into practice when someone else disagrees with you about a topic important to you?**

Young-Teenager Tip:
JR. HIGH MINISTRY Magazine reports "the average teenager watches 2 hours, 43 minutes (of television) each day."

Say: **Today we're going to do a project to help us understand how we can all look at the same object but have a different point of view about it.**

Give each student two cardboard tubes. Tell kids to tape the two tubes together, one next to the other, with masking tape, to form binoculars. Then have kids create lenses for their cardboard binoculars using the supplies you've provided.

For example, kids might cover the ends of their tubes with colored plastic or with paper that has a zillion pin-pricked holes in it. Kids might also attach paper that has hole-punched holes, or attach small strips of paper running horizontally or vertically or diagonally (or a combination of the three). See the diagram below for ideas.

On the other end of their binoculars, have kids hole-punch one hole on the outer side of each tube. Give each student a 2-foot length of yarn and instruct kids to tie the ends of the yarn to the binoculars through the holes.

Have kids form pairs, then take everyone outside. Tell kids to choose a partner who made different lenses for his or her binoculars. Then instruct kids to walk side by side, look through their binoculars, and describe what they see through their filtered glasses. Have kids focus on and describe one or two specific objects, such as a car or the church steeple.

Have kids gather for discussion and ask: **How were your perspectives on the same objects similar to or different from each other? What was it like** to hear that someone saw something differently than you? When do you face this in your everyday living? How do you handle it when you see a situation differently than someone else? How can we view things differently but still have unity?

Scriptures for Deeper Study: John 10:16; 1 Corinthians 1:10; 12:12-13; 1 Peter 3:8.

World's Largest Paper Airplane

Focus of the Fun: Kids create and attempt to fly a huge paper airplane, then discuss how God is not limited by what is possible to humans.

Supplies: Butcher paper or newsprint, scissors, masking tape, and one Bible per student. You may also want about 20 sheets of paper.

Tell kids to take off their shoes and leave them near the door of the room. Have the group cover the floor of the youth room with butcher paper (or newsprint), by rolling paper onto the floor against one wall from one end to the other, cutting it, then rolling another piece next to the first piece, and continuing until they've reached the opposite wall.

Make sure that the strips of paper overlap each other by half an inch. Then have kids tape the pieces together with masking tape running the length of each piece of paper. When the group has taped one side, flip the whole piece over and tape the edges together on that side.

Have the group collaborate to design a gigantic paper airplane, sharing their paper-airplane construction techniques. Have them test out some of their ideas with 8½×11-inch paper. When the group has decided how to design the giant airplane, have kids fold their huge piece of paper accordingly.

Before attempting to launch the airplane, ask: **On a possibility scale of 1 to 1,023, how possible do you think it is to fly this plane? Explain.** Then take the plane outside to your church parking lot or a nearby park and give it a few test runs. Allow five runs to see how far the plane will fly. Let kids change the plane design between runs to see if they can make it more aerodynamic.

Ask: **How accurate was your guess about the possibility of flying this plane?** Have the group read Matthew 19:26 in unison. Ask: **What kinds of things in your life seem impossible that you now know are possible with God?**

Young-Teenager Tip: Gerald W. Bracey, research psychologist and education consultant, reports on an individual's perceived nerdiness in his article "From Normal to Nerd—and Back Again." Bracey found that high school students looking back on their middle school years felt that "80% of the (middle school) population were nerds or dweebs, while 20% were trendies." This means that four out of five of your students may feel unpopular or unlikeable, so give them lots of encouragement! (There is hope. Bracey also reports that many students who perceived themselves as nerds in middle school identified themselves as normal in high school.) (Gerald W. Bracey, "From Normal to Nerd—and Back Again," Phi Delta Kappan)

Scriptures for Deeper Study: Mark 9:14-24; Luke 1:26-37.

2 Small-Group Projects

Tired of the same old question-and-answer format for small-group learning? Why not build or bake something instead? Use the projects in this chapter to involve a small group of up to 12 students in creating a tangible object that illustrates a Scriptural message.

TIME FOCUS: VARIES ACCORDING TO PROJECT.

NUMBER OF STUDENTS: TWO TO 12.

Balloon Games

Focus of the Fun: Junior highers will explore how God uses people in different ways, as they create unique games using balloons and other basic supplies.

Supplies: Balloons, tape, pencils, cardboard, poster board, markers, and Bibles.

Form teams of no more than three. Give each team a supply of balloons, tape, pencils, and cardboard. Say: **Work in your team to design a game that uses your supplies in unique ways. Discuss with each other what kind of game you want to create, then prepare the supplies accordingly. Try to come up with a game that's uniquely yours and isn't simply a variation on a familiar game.**

Give groups up to 30 minutes to design and prepare their games. Have kids list the rules for their games on poster board for all to see. When groups are ready, have them take turns explaining and leading the whole group in playing their games.

Afterward, form a circle and have kids read aloud 1 Corinthians 12:1-31. Ask: **How is the variety of games we played like the variety of gifts represented in our group? Why is it important to have variety in gifts and abilities? What did you learn about each other's abilities and gifts during this activity? How can we support one another's gifts and abilities?**

Scriptures for Deeper Study: Romans 12:3-8; 14:1-23; 15:7-13.

Boats Afloat

Focus of the Fun: Kids create "seaworthy" boats and learn about trusting God during life's storms.

Supplies: Aluminum foil, string, paper, masking tape, glue, paper clips, newspaper, cardboard, paper or plastic cups, yarn, craft sticks, toothpicks, rubber bands, and any other materials you want to offer for building a small boat. You'll also need one Bible per student.

Arrange to hold the meeting in a place that has a baby pool, bathtub, or a large sink. Before the meeting, fill the bathtub or sink two-thirds full with water.

Say: **Choose something you have on you or with you today that you don't mind getting wet. For example, you could choose a ring, a shoelace, or a penny.** When kids have chosen their items, say: **Today we are going to make water vehicles to carry your items from one end of a bathtub** (or sink) **to the other. You can use any of the items I've provided to create your boat, raft, or other contraption. Keep in mind that you will not be able to put your hands in the water to propel your water vehicle, so provide some other means of moving your craft. For instance, you could make a sail to blow on or figure out some way to launch your craft with rubber bands.**

Give students 30 minutes to create their boats, rafts, or other vehicles. When kids have finished creating their boats, go to the bathtub or sink and have kids test their inventions. Yell "Go!" and have kids launch their contraptions. Make waves with your hands to make the task harder. Or stir the water in one direction to create a whirlpool.

After these races, ask: **How much did you trust your water vehicle to transport your item across the tub** (sink)**? What would you trust to get your item safely to the other side? Why?**

Have the group read Matthew 14:22-33 aloud, with each person reading one verse, going around the group until the passage has been completed. Ask: **How is this story like today's project? How would you respond if you were in Peter's shoes? What do you think made Peter stop looking at Jesus? What is one situation in your life right now in which you need to keep looking at Jesus? How can you remember to trust Jesus in that situation?**

Variation: For a summer-day project, have your small group collaborate to build a contraption that can transport a person across a pool without using the person's arms or legs directly as propulsion. In other words, kids can't use swimming motions such as paddling or kicking, but they can use oars. For example, the group could inflate an inner tube around the frame of an old bicycle, tie the inner tube to the frame with twine, attach flippers to the tires, and have riders pedal their way across the pool.

Have half the group stand on one side of the pool and the other half on the other side. Have one person from the first side propel the craft across the pool, then one person from the other side cross back. Continue until everyone is on the side opposite from where they started. Ask: **How much did you trust your contraption to safely transport you across the pool? What would you have trusted in more? Why? How is this activity like the story of Peter trying to walk on water toward Christ?**

Scriptures for Deeper Study: Matthew 6:25-34; 8:23-27.

Bridge Building

Focus of the Fun: Kids learn about building relationships by building a bridge.

Supplies: You'll need to provide two chairs of the same size, an empty 2-liter plastic bottle, two pieces of paper, two pencils, and two Bibles. In addition, kids may gather any supplies they can find.

Form two groups (a group can be one person). Give each group a chair and have the groups pick a place to set their chairs. They may choose any location—in a driveway, in two rooms connected by a doorway, or in the same room—as long as the two chairs are 5 feet apart.

Young-Teenager Tip: Most junior high boys will spend the majority of their free time in one of two pursuits: playing sports or playing video games. Junior high boys simply enjoy playing—period. Get their attention by sponsoring fun nights just for them.

Say: **We're going to build a bridge between the chairs. Both groups must work to build a bridge toward each other. You can use anything around this place to build your bridge, and you can cooperate between groups to build the bridge. However, you cannot walk between the chairs to give supplies to each other. The goal is to be able to roll this bottle across the bridge to each other.**

Allow kids 45 minutes to create their bridge. They may use anything they can find that they won't be able to damage. Some suggestions are broom handles, string, cardboard, and newspaper.

When the two groups have built the bridge, give each group a piece of paper and a pencil. Have each group write an affirmation message about working with the other group. For example, one group could write, "Thanks for thinking of an inventive way to support our bridge." Then give one group the empty 2-liter plastic bottle and tell the group members to fold their message, stuff it into the opening of the bottle, and roll the bottle across the bridge. When the bottle reaches the other group, have those group members take the message out, read it, and then put their message into the bottle and roll it back to the first group. Have the first group read the message.

Ask: **What does it take to build a bridge between two groups? What inner resources did you have to use? How did you feel when you completed the task? How did you feel in being able to transport a message to one another? How was building this bridge like building a friendship with someone?**

Have both groups open Bibles to Philippians 2:1-4. Have each group read two verses aloud. Then ask: **What do these verses say about building relationships with others? What kinds of "supplies" do you need to build a friendship?**

Variation: If you know of a nearby stream, have your group build a bridge from one side of the stream to the other. Be sure that students can get safely to both sides of the stream to do the project. You will also need drivers and vehicles to transport kids and supplies to the stream.

Scriptures for Deeper Study: 1 Samuel 18:1-4; John 15:12-17; Philippians 2:19-23.

Can Castle

Focus of the Fun: Kids will get a glimpse of heaven's grandeur as they build a huge castle using aluminum cans and duct tape.

Supplies: Empty aluminum cans, duct tape, and Bibles. Optional: a book with pictures of castles.

Long before you attempt this activity, you may want to announce in church that you need aluminum cans. To make this activity work as well as possible, you'll need hundreds of aluminum cans for kids to use—the more the better.

Give kids a huge supply of empty aluminum cans and a roll or two of duct tape. Have the kids build a "can castle" by taping the empty cans together to form walls, turrets, doors, windows, and other parts of a castle. To help with the building, you might want to have an illustrated book of castles for kids to look at.

Young-Teenager Tip: Eleven percent of American crimes are committed by people under the age of 15. (*100% American* by Daniel Evan Weiss)

Have kids build the castle in one meeting or over a long period of time (adding cans as they're available). The goal of this activity is to create a huge, awe-inspiring building; so the more kids add to the construction, the better.

When the castle is finished, have kids sit near it (or inside it, if they really did some impressive work). Have volunteers read aloud John 14:2-3 and Revelation 21:1-4. Then ask: **How is this grand castle like a glimpse of heaven? What are you looking forward to most about heaven? How is the way we've worked on this castle like the way we live our lives in anticipation of a future home in heaven?**

After kids tire of the castle, have them dismantle the work of art and recycle the aluminum cans at a local recycling center.

Scriptures for Deeper Study: 2 Chronicles 2:6; Isaiah 66:1; 2 Peter 3:13.

The Future Machine

Focus of the Fun: Kids will create a "time machine" and dream about their futures.

Supplies: Bibles, large cardboard boxes, wire, miscellaneous electrical supplies, duct tape, and other construction materials.

Place all the supplies in the middle of a large room. If there are more than 10 kids in the group, consider having two or more groups do the project simultaneously in different rooms.

Say: **We're going to look into our future during this project. But first, we'll need a time machine to see what the future looks like.**

Have kids work together to construct their version of a time machine using the cardboard boxes and miscellaneous items. Explain that there are only two rules for construction:

1. A person must be able to enter and sit or stand in the machine.

2. The person in the machine must have a viewing screen (cutout section) in the time machine.

Allow kids plenty of time to have fun creating their machine. Then have kids take turns getting into the time machine. After someone's in the machine, have the rest of the kids brainstorm what they think that person's future might be like. Remind kids to come up with only positive future options. Then have volunteers act out that future for the person in the machine to see through the viewing screen. After all kids have had a turn seeing their futures, form pairs and have them read Ecclesiastes 7:14 and 8:7. Ask: **What can we truly know about our futures? What role does our faith in God play in our futures? How can we shape our futures by what we do today? What scares you most about the future? What excites you most?**

To close, have kids take turns telling each other one thing they look forward to about each other's future.

Scriptures for Deeper Study: Jeremiah 29:10-14; 31:16-17; Proverbs 23:17-18.

Gifts

Focus of the Fun: Kids will experience the act of gift-giving as they create personalized gifts for each other.

Supplies: Cardboard, tape, paper, pencils, wrapping paper and ribbons, Bibles, and items as determined by group members.

For this project, you will need an adult driver for every group.

Form groups of no more than four (groups can be as small as one person). Then pair up groups and have them sit near each other. Say: **The group you are paired with is your "partner group." You are responsible for getting to know the interests of the people in your partner group. A good way to do this is to ask each other questions such as "What are your favorite hobbies? What foods do you like best? If you could do anything you wanted for a whole year, what would it be?"**

Provide paper and pencils so kids can make notes about their "partner group" members' interests. Allow 15 to 30 minutes for kids to talk with one another and get to know one another.

After time is up, send groups out with an adult driver on a mission to collect items for a personalized gift they'll create for their partner group. Kids can go to homes, stores, or any other place they choose. For example, kids might collect baseball cards, candy bars, comics, and lip gloss for a group whose members like those items. Provide cardboard and tape so groups can piece together the items they collect to create a single gift to present to their partner group. (**Note:** If kids want to spend money buying items for their gifts, set a spending limit of no more than $5 per group.)

When the gifts are completed (kids may want to wrap them or put ribbons on them), have each group make a presentation to its partner group in front of the whole group. Encourage kids to explain why they chose each item in the gift and what it represents about the individual's interests.

When all the gifts have been presented, have partner groups sit together to read John 3:16-18 and discuss the following questions: **What did you like about giving gifts to each other? What was it like to receive gifts from each other? How do the feelings you had in this activity compare to the way we feel about the greatest gift of all—God sending his Son to die for us? What was your response to the gifts you were given today? What should our response be to God's gift of eternal life?**

Scriptures for Deeper Study: Ephesians 2:8; Matthew 7:7-11.

Locomotion

Focus of the Fun: Kids will create a cardboard train and train track and discuss the qualities of leaders worth following.

Supplies: For each person (including yourself), you'll need one shoe box, three shoe-box lids, two paper clips, four 1½-inch nails, four jar lids (each set of four jar lids must be the same size, but each person can have a different-size set), and one jar that the lids will fit on. You'll also need masking tape, a hammer, colorful markers, stickers, old magazines, scissors, glue, glitter, and any other decorative materials you wish to make available to your kids. Also provide one Bible per student.

Say: **We are going to create our own electric-train substitute together.** Give each student one shoe box, four jar lids, four nails, and two paper clips. As the leader, you will also create a train car out of these materials. Your car will be used as the engine car in front of the train.

Have kids attach wheels (jar lids) to the train car (shoe box) by completing the following steps:

1. Poke a hole in the center of each lid by hammering a nail into the center of the lid. (To do this safely, have kids screw the lid to a jar before they hammer the nail into the lid.)

2. Punch the nails (with the lids attached) through the shoe box (punching from outside to inside) at both ends of the long sides of the box where the bottom and the side of the box meet. (See diagram page 30.)

3. Tape the part of the nails inside the box to the bottom of the box, leaving enough nail space outside to allow the jar lids to spin.

Next have kids form the connections between train cars with the following steps.

4. Open the paper clips to create an S shape.

5. Poke two holes the width of the paper clip in the center of the narrow part of the box.

6. Thread the paper clip through the holes so that one curved part of the S in the paper clip is pulled through.

Young-Teenager Tip: Junior highers go through numerous emotions at a rapid pace. To help you determine where any particular student is at any one time, ask him or her to rate how he or she feels on a scale from 1 to 137 (or any other number you choose) and why. This can give you a sense of where your student is emotionally. Students respond positively when they believe someone understands their feelings.

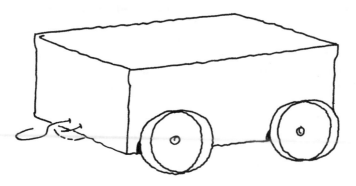

Have kids repeat this process on the other narrow side of the box.

Then, have kids create a train track out of the shoe-box lids following these directions.

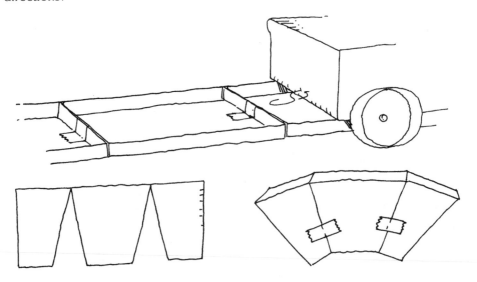

7. Place the box lids flat side down on the floor. The lips on the box lids are now the rails. Put the train cars on the lids with the wheels outside the rails to make sure that the wheels reach the floor. If the rails are too high, trim them.

8. Arrange the box lids on the floor to create a track. Tape the lids to the floor as you line them up and tape all of the lids together along the sides.

9. Create railroad ties by taping pieces of masking tape across the lids to help retain the shape of the lids.

10. To create turns, cut one or two V-shaped darts out of one long side of a lid. Then tape the sides of the darts together with masking tape.

When kids have finished constructing their cars and the train track, say: **Now that you have your cars constructed, decorate them in such a way that describes who you are. You can draw on them, glue pictures from these magazines on them, and fill the cars in any way you like. For example, if you like tennis, find a picture of a tennis racket and paste it on the outside of your car or place it inside your car.**

When all the cars are finished, have your students connect them by putting one end of their paper clip S into another person's paper clip S. Make sure everyone's train car is connected to someone else's. Put your engine car in the front of the train. Take the train for a test run along the track.

After the test run, ask: **What pulled the train along the track? Once you connected your car to the train, how could you determine where your car would go?** Say: **Every train needs an engine to pull and guide it safely along the way.**

Have kids read John 10:1-6 to themselves. Ask: **How is Jesus Christ as a shepherd like the engine of our train? What kind of qualities does Jesus have that make him a good leader? How can we use his example to find worthy leaders to follow today?**

Ask: **What qualities do you look for in a leader?** Allow kids to find pictures and decorate the engine with characteristics that they want in a leader. For example, they may wish to put a compact Bible into the engine.

Scriptures for Deeper Study: Exodus 13:21-22; Joshua 1:6-9; Psalms 5:8; 27:11; 78:52-53; Isaiah 40:11; 42:16.

Mascots

Focus of the Fun: Junior highers will explore what it means to be Christlike as they create a larger-than-life mascot for their group that represents Christlike characteristics.

Supplies: Bibles, paper, pencils, chicken wire, duct tape, and various colors of tissue paper.

Have junior highers read aloud the following Scripture passages: Romans 15:1-6; 1 Corinthians 10:31–11:1; Ephesians 4:32; 5:1-2; and Philippians 2:5-11.

Then ask: **What do these passages tell us about Christ's character? What do they tell us about how we should live out our faith? Which Christlike characteristics do you find most difficult to live out?**

Have kids list Christlike characteristics on a sheet of paper, then choose one or two that represent the nature of your group. For example, if your group is especially caring, they might choose "compassion"; if they're quick to forgive, they might choose "forgiveness."

Then say: **We're going to create a mascot or group symbol that represents the Christlike characteristics we've chosen that best describe our group.**

Form groups of no more than three and have each group brainstorm a mascot or symbol they'd like to use to represent their Christlike characteristics. For example, a mascot for a caring group might be a big, huggable bear. Or a symbol for a loving group might be a big heart.

Have kids vote on the mascot or symbol they like best, then have them work together to make a larger-than-life model of their mascot or symbol (like the kind you might find on a parade float). First have kids design the mascot or symbol on paper. Then have them use the chicken wire and duct tape to form the body shape. Twist flowers out of tissue paper and tuck them in the openings of the chicken wire for the finished effect.

When the mascot is completed, display it in the meeting room or church as a lasting reminder of the group's Christlike character and the goal of becoming more Christlike.

Scriptures for Deeper Study: 1 Peter 4:13; Colossians 1:15-23.

The Not-Far-Away "Family" Vacation

Focus of the Fun: Kids learn about belonging to the family of God by taking a one-day "family" vacation together.

Supplies: An instant-print camera and one package of film, a piece of poster board, tape, an assortment of felt-tip pens, and Bibles.

Before the meeting, arrange for enough drivers to transport the group around the community. Tell kids to come dressed and packed for their favorite vacation. For example, some kids may bring ski equipment while others may bring bathing suits and beach towels.

When kids arrive, say: **We are going on a "family" vacation today, and we are going to be a family together. So let's decide where we are going, who is Mom, who is Dad, and who are brothers and sisters.**

Have kids develop an itinerary of local spots where they can take pictures of their "family" on vacation. For example, go to a local swimming pool and have kids sunbathe, swim, or read by the pool. Then go to a nearby hill and have the skiers pose.

Have kids play their roles both in the pictures and during transportation. For example, kids acting as brothers and sisters can argue over one person taking too much space and complain that they need to go to the bathroom. Dad can pretend to get lost and not stop for directions, and Mom can try to keep things under control.

While transporting the kids, ask them to share stories about their favorite family vacations.

Return to the meeting place. Have kids tape the pictures to the poster board and write captions underneath to create a photo album of their "vacation."

Ask: **What is it like to go on a vacation with your family? What are some other things that families do together besides go on vacations? What does the word "family" mean to you?**

Have kids read aloud Luke 8:19-21 in unison. Ask: **What does Jesus say about his family? How can we be part of God's family? What does it mean to be brothers and sisters in Christ?**

Scriptures for Deeper Study: Romans 12:10; 1 Thessalonians 4:9-10; Hebrews 13:1; James 2:15-16; 1 John 4:19-21.

Focus of the Fun: Junior highers will examine their priorities as they create rocket ships and fill them with items that represent what's important in life.

Supplies: You'll need to provide refrigerator boxes, markers, duct tape, scissors or utility knives, and Bibles. In addition, kids will collect items of their own choosing.

(You'll need to have an adult driver for every group)

Form groups of no more than four and instruct each group to make a rocket ship, using the supplies you've provided.

Say: **What would you take with you if you were going on an expedition to the stars and knew you'd never be coming back? As you work on your rocket ships, think about what kinds of things you'd take with you. When the ships are complete, we'll actually collect as many of these items as possible and place them in our ships.**

When the rockets are done, have kids go with adult drivers to collect the items they thought of (each group should come up with its list independently). It's OK if junior highers place one item in the box to represent a number of items (a box of cookies to represent food or a T-shirt to represent clothing). Then have groups place the items in their ships and make "cargo lists" of the items on the outside of the boxes so everyone can read what's included. Have groups explain what's inside their rocket ships and why they decided to take those items.

Then read aloud Colossians 3:1-17. Ask: **How did you determine what was most important to take along on this trip? What determines what's most important in our lives? What does Colossians 3:2 have to say about our priorities in life? How can the message of Colossians help us set priorities?**

Display the rocket ships in the youth group room for a couple weeks as reminders that we're to set our minds on heavenly things.

Scriptures for Deeper Study: Romans 12:2; 2 Peter 3:13; John 14:2-3.

Operation: Imitation

Focus of the Fun: Kids will explore what it means to imitate Christ as they interview church members.

Supplies: A video camera, a videotape, a church directory, paper, pencils, a stack of your business cards and Bibles. Also set up a television with a VCR.

rrange transportation for the whole group.

Say: **Today we're going to survey members of our church about people they want to be like.** Help kids create a brief survey. Some sample survey questions might be:
- Who would you most want to be like?
- What is it about that person that would make you want to imitate that person?
- If you were to imitate that person, how would you go about it?

When the group has constructed its survey questions, pack the kids, the video camera and videotape, pencils, and photocopies of the survey into the church van or car. Be sure to bring the church directory and your business cards. Have kids choose someone from the church that they would like to interview, then drive to that person's house.

At each house, have kids introduce themselves and explain that they are from the church. Hand the person one of your cards and ask permission to interview them briefly for a survey. If the respondent is willing, have someone record the survey interview on videotape.

Interview about 10 people, and then return to the meeting place to watch the video and go through the survey answers. Ask: **What kinds of people did others want to imitate? How do you imitate someone? Who would you like to imitate?**

Have the group read Ephesians 5:1 aloud in unison. Ask: **How can we imitate God? What kinds of things about him should we imitate? What is one way you will imitate him this week?**

Scriptures for Deeper Study: 1 Thessalonians 1:6-7; Hebrews 6:12; 3 John 11.

Our Magazine

Focus of the Fun: Kids will learn about each other as they create a magazine describing the group members.

Supplies: Poster board or newsprint, markers, photographs of group members, a variety of magazines, tape, and Bibles.

Before this activity, ask group members to bring photographs of themselves to the meeting. Or plan on having an instant-print camera on hand to use during the activity.

Form groups of no more than five. Say: **The object of this activity is to create a magazine that describes the people in your group in creative ways. You may want to pattern your magazine after an actual magazine by using the same logo style, similar columns, or article ideas. But the magazine you create must tell us about the members of your group. You can use pictures, markers, tape, and other supplies as needed to create your magazine.**

If kids are especially creative, consider having them create a magazine at least 12 pages long (they can write in large print to fill the space if they like). Otherwise, a magazine of six pages is fine. Pass out the real magazines to give kids ideas on how to create their own magazine identity. For example, kids who choose to pattern their magazine after a movie magazine might include "movie reviews" that are actually articles about the various group members. A "top 10" list for films might list the group members' favorites. And a "coming soon" section might list upcoming activities the group members are planning.

Encourage creativity and allow plenty of time for groups to create their magazines. For added fun, make a rule that kids can't write articles about themselves—someone else in the group must write about them.

When the magazines are finished, pass them around so kids can read them.

Then read aloud 1 Corinthians 8:1-3 and Jeremiah 1:5 and discuss the following questions: **How does this activity help us know each other better? What do the Scriptures tell us about how God knows us? What kind of magazine might God create describing your group members? What articles would God write about your life? How can we get to know God better?**

Scriptures for Deeper Study: Psalm 139; John 10:7-18.

Paper Trails

Focus of the Fun: Kids will create a huge paper strip and explore the role perseverance plays in following God.

Supplies: Scrap paper, tape, staplers, and Bibles.

Before the event, tell group members they're going to create a huge ribbon to encircle the church (or another designated building). For several weeks, have group members collect scrap paper from a variety of locations. Junior highers may collect paper from trash bins, from people who live near the church, or from their own homes. The object of the activity is to collect enough paper to completely encircle the building. This activity works best if it is done over the course of a few weeks. Have kids collect paper and bring it to group meetings each week.

Encourage kids to collect all kinds of paper (including trash they find on the street). Store the paper in a corner of the meeting room until kids think they have enough to encircle the church.

When kids are ready to create their large "ribbon" around the church, help them begin taping and stapling the papers together until they have long strips to take outside and piece together into one huge circle. Because paper tears easily, kids will probably have to repair torn areas until they've successfully encircled the church.

When the paper is surrounding the church, take a few photographs to record the event for posterity. Then have kids gather near the paper ribbon.

Have someone read aloud Exodus 3:1-14; 4:1, 13-17. Then discuss the following questions: **What were your first reactions when you learned about this project? What were your feelings as you saw this project progress** (or not progress)**? How is the way we approached this activity like the way Moses responded to God's call for him to lead the Israelites out of Egypt? How are the results similar? How are they different? How did our perseverance affect the outcome of this activity? What can we learn from Moses' example of perseverance to help us in everyday situations? What are ways perseverance helps us grow in faith?**

Young-Teenager Tip: Encourage one student each day! Print out self-adhesive address labels (either by computer or by hand) for every student in your junior high group. Then put all the labels in an empty, clean jar. Each day pull out one label, pray for that student, and write an encouraging message to him or her on the back of a postcard. For example, "Katie, I prayed for you today! I hope you do well in your cheerleading tryouts!" Affix the label to the other side of the postcard, put a stamp on the postcard, and mail it. Continue this every day until your jar is empty.

Scriptures for Deeper Study: Matthew 28:16-20; Mark 16:14-18.

Perspectives

Focus of the Fun: Kids will learn about seeing things through others' eyes as they create visual depictions of things from a variety of perspectives.

Supplies: Poster board, cardboard, paper, tape, glue, markers, scissors, and Bibles.

ave volunteers read aloud John 4:1-30. Then ask: **What impact did Jesus' conversation with the Samaritan woman have on her life? Since Jews weren't supposed to associate with Samaritans, how would the impact have been different if Jesus had followed the custom of the day and not spoken to the woman? How did Jesus' ability to see the woman from a different perspective help him communicate truth to her? Why is it important to see people from a variety of perspectives?**

Form groups of no more than four (a group can be one person) and give each group a large sheet of poster board, a supply of cardboard, paper, tape, glue, scissors, and markers. Say: **I'm going to assign each of you a different "perspective" of the world, and then give you an assignment to create a three-dimensional picture using that perspective. In other words, you're to create a picture in a way that illustrates how your assigned person or creature would see the world. Don't tell the other groups your assignment.**

Assign each group a different perspective from the following list (or come up with your own):
- a child's perspective,
- a dog's perspective,
- a fish's perspective,
- an ant's perspective,
- an elderly person's perspective, or
- a rock 'n' roller's perspective.

Have groups create their three-dimensional pictures by cutting out cardboard shapes and taping them onto a poster-board base to represent the elements they'd "see" from their assigned perspective. Encourage kids to think about what they'd see, think, feel, and experience from their assigned perspectives.

After the three-dimensional pictures are complete, have groups guess what perspective is represented by other groups' pictures. Then discuss what this activity teaches about understanding different points of view.

Scriptures for Deeper Study: Matthew 6:22-23; 1 Corinthians 12:5-28; Ephesians 4:32.

The Praise God Tour

Focus of the Fun: Kids will develop a creative presentation for leading others in praise.

Supplies: One Bible for every two people. Other supplies to be decided by the group.

orm pairs. Have the group read Psalm 150 with each pair reading one verse aloud until the group has read the whole psalm. Ask: **What does this psalm say to you about praising God? What are some ways you can praise God every day? What are some unusual, creative ways we can praise God together and share our praise with others?**

Have kids brainstorm a way that the whole group can put together a praise performance. One idea would be to create a band with the musical talents in the group. Have the group choose a praise song they like, practice it, and "tour" to Sunday school classes to share their praise. Get permission from Sunday school classes to come in and perform. Or have kids practice five or six praise songs and tour to other youth groups in the area.

Another idea would be to develop a puppet band. Have the kids create puppets out of old socks, buttons, yarn, glue, markers, and beady eyes (available at craft stores). Create a puppet theater by draping a queen-size sheet over an 8-foot rectangular table, set horizontally against the ground. Have kids hide behind the table and show the puppets over the top edge. The group could create a praise puppet show with a plot; they could be a puppet choir and sing a praise song; or they could create a puppet music video, playing a praise song by their favorite Christian artists like The Newsboys or DC Talk and having the puppets lip-sync.

Other ideas for touring groups include: a dance group (create a dance to a favorite praise song); a drama group (develop a skit that communicates the importance of praise); a clown band (have kids dress up in colorful, baggy clothes, put on clown makeup from a costume store, find fun music, and develop a funny praise routine); a pantomime group (dress in all black, wear clown makeup, and have kids mime a praise to God); or an acrobat group (have kids make an acrobatic formation and recite Psalm 150:6 while in that stance).

Scriptures for Deeper Study: 1 Chronicles 29:10-13; Psalms 21:13; 89:5; 138:2; 146:1-2; 147:1; 148.

Weight Lifting

Focus of the Fun: Kids will create a machine to lift heavy objects and discuss how Jesus lifts the weight of our sins.

Supplies: Two 1×6×6-foot boards, three rolling pins (or wooden cylinders), and masking tape. You also will need up to five things of different weights (for example, a folding chair, a bicycle, or a box full of books). Don't use anything that could be damaged if dropped and don't lift people. Gather one Bible for every two people.

ut the objects to be lifted in the middle of the meeting room. When kids arrive, say: **We need to develop a machine to lift these objects one at a time. We can use people to operate the machine, but no one may touch the objects while they are being lifted—in other words, no lifting them or steadying them with our hands.**

Allow the group time to create a lever system, using one or more rolling pins, one or more of the boards, and the masking tape. Give kids the opportunity to test their lever system with the smallest object first. When kids have successfully lifted the smallest object, move to the next object in line and have kids use their lever system to lift that one. Continue until they have lifted each object or they've met with an object the group's lever system could not lift.

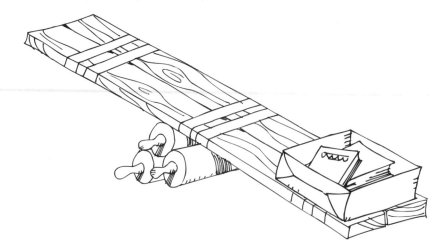

Afterward, ask: **How was it to try to lift these objects without touching them ourselves? What are some things we couldn't lift even if we could use our hands? What are some situations in our lives that seem too big for us to carry on our own?**

Have kids form pairs. Have pairs read 1 Peter 2:24-25. Ask: **How is this passage like our weight lifting activity today? What does it take to lift the weight of our sins from our shoulders? What is our part in this process? What is Jesus' part?**

Scriptures for Deeper Study: Romans 3:23-24; 6:23; 7:21-25; 2 Corinthians 5:21; Hebrews 7:23-28.

Worship Centers

Focus of the Fun: Junior highers will design worship centers for the youth group and congregation and explore what it means to worship.

Supplies: You'll need to provide curtains or sheets, scissors, tape, paper, markers, and Bibles. In addition, kids will gather supplies they wish to use.

Form groups of no more than five and have each group design and decorate a "worship center" based on a specific theme (for example, family, Jesus' sacrifice, God's love, Creation). Assign each group a specific area in your meeting room (or another room designated to house the worship centers) and allow kids to hang curtains or use furniture to separate the worship centers.

Encourage groups to refer to the following Scripture passages as they consider the theme they'll use for their worship centers: Psalms 23; 104; 150; Luke 22:14-22; 1 Timothy 1:12-17; Revelation 19:11-16.

Ask groups to decorate their worship centers to match their chosen themes. They may use the supplies you've provided and gather other objects from around the meeting area. Tell kids how long their centers will be in place (ideally at least a month), so they can choose items that will last that long and won't need to be returned immediately. For instance, a group with the theme "Creation" might tape lots of pictures of God's creation around the center and place a plant or flowers in the room.

Have each group write a worship suggestion list based on its theme that people can follow when they enter the worship center to worship God. For example, a group with a worship center based on the family might have a list that includes the following items.

- Think of three things about your family you're thankful for.
- Ask God to heal the hurts in your family.
- Praise God for being the ultimate "parent" for all Christians.

After the worship centers are complete, have kids introduce them to each other and to the whole congregation. Encourage youth group members and congregation members to spend some time in each of the worship centers during the coming weeks. If possible, keep the centers up for at least a month.

Scriptures for Deeper Study: Psalms 75; 95; 103; 145; Philippians 2:10-11.

X-Ray Vision

Focus of the Fun: Kids will make an "X-ray machine" to illustrate that God loves us for who we are inside.

Supplies: Bibles, paper, markers, blank transparencies, markers usable on transparencies, tape, an overhead projector, and a collapsible movie screen.

Do this project with a group of students who already know one another and feel comfortable with one another.

Before the group arrives, set up the overhead projector and screen. Set up the screen so the top of the screen is at the height of your average junior higher's neck (so kids can see over it). You may need to adjust it during the activity for the varying heights of your students. Then set up the overhead projector to fill up the screen as much as possible when lit. On a transparency, draw an upper-body outline in black marker (see diagram below). Place this transparency on the overhead projector glass.

Form pairs. Have pairs read 1 Samuel 16:1-8 to each other. Ask: **How did Samuel try to find a king for Israel? How did God want Samuel to determine the next king? What does this story say about how we should look at people? How do you share with someone who you are on the inside?**

Say: **Today we are going to do an X-ray examination of each of us. We are going to have an opportunity to see each other's insides and discover what's there. But first, we are going to take a look at who we are on the outside.** Give each student a sheet of paper and markers. Instruct the group to draw or write, in a descriptive way, the kind of image they want others to have of them.

When the kids have finished their "outside" pictures, give each student a transparency and say: **On this transparency, draw a picture or write some words that express who you feel you are on the inside, the part that not many people know.** Give the group some time to complete this part of the project. As kids finish, have them tape their outside picture on top of the transparency, using a strip of tape across the top of both pictures. Have each person tape the paper and transparency together on one side only.

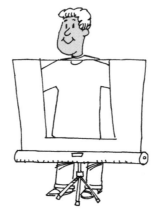

Have each student hold up and explain his or her outside picture to the group. Then have that student move behind the "X-ray machine" (the movie screen). Put his or her picture and transparency over the upper-body outline transparency. Then flip the student's outside picture off of his or her inside transparency, projecting the inside picture onto the screen.

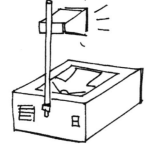

Ask the group: **What do you see about this person that you didn't know before?** Have every member of the group share both pictures, going behind the "X-ray machine" to share the inside picture.

Ask: **How does it feel to share who you are on the inside? When do you share your inside self with others? When, if ever, is it not a good idea to share our inside self?**

Say: **You all have been courageous to share your insides with the rest of us today.**

Scriptures for Deeper Study: 1 Kings 8:39; 1 Chronicles 29:9; Psalm 139:1-4; 139:23-24.

3 Saturday Projects

Remember spending all Saturday morning eating Cap'n Crunch and watching cartoons until your eyeballs ached? Those were the days and your young teenagers know them well. Remember how it took something extra special to entice you into forsaking the tradition? Well, here is primo enticement material. Saturday Projects are super-fun projects that take all day or may even include an overnighter or traveling to exotic locations! Saturday will never be the same again.

TIME FOCUS: AN AFTERNOON, A FULL DAY, OR OVERNIGHT.

NUMBER OF STUDENTS: UNLIMITED.

(**Note:** You'll probably want to line up transportation for many of the projects in this chapter.)

Altar of Bricks

Focus of the Fun: Kids will use bricks and mortar to create an altar, then place something of value inside the altar as a symbol of their obedience to God.

Supplies: Bricks, mortar, trowels, plywood, saw, and Bibles.

Before the activity, invite group members to bring an object that represents something important in their lives (such as a picture of a sport they enjoy or a letter from a friend). Let kids know that the object won't be returned after the activity.

When kids arrive, have them help design a simple, closed-box altar to be built out of bricks, mortar, and a sheet of plywood. To design the box, kids might draw on paper or arrange the bricks without mortar to see what the final product might look like.

Take the supplies to a site where the altar can remain permanently and have kids build it together. If you have a large group, have kids work in shifts, allowing each person a chance to place bricks or spread the mortar. Let this be the kids' project (give as little advice as possible). After kids have formed the walls of the altar and cut a piece of plywood to fit the top, have them stop working and take a break.

Form a circle around the nearly completed altar and have volunteers read aloud Genesis 22:1-14. Have kids tell about the items they brought and what they represent. Have kids take the items and place them inside the altar. Then have volunteers place the mortar around the top of the altar and cover it with the plywood top.

Ask: **How is our symbolic act like what Abraham did? How is it unlike Abraham? Is it easy or difficult to submit to God's will? How might you have acted in Abraham's place? In Isaac's place? What can we do to show we want to obey God in our lives? What are specific ways we can offer our gifts, talents, and interests to God? How would God want us to treat our gifts, talents, and interests?**

Leave the altar in place as long as possible to remind junior highers how Abraham obeyed God and how they're to obey God in all areas of their lives.

Scriptures for Deeper Study: Genesis 8:20-21; Exodus 17:15-16; and Deuteronomy 27:4-10.

Back in Time

Focus of the Fun: Young teenagers will decorate the church as it might have looked 100 years ago, then participate in a worship service celebrating their heritage of faith.

Supplies: Old clothes, pictures of a church from about 100 years ago, a variety of old books, furniture, and other items, and Bibles.

If your church has a long and rich heritage, track down pictures of the church and its people from many years ago (as many as 100, if possible). If your church is relatively young, visit a local library and check out a few books that include pictures of the way people dressed many years ago (and what a church might've looked like back then).

Young-Teenager Tip:
Running out of possibilities for adult leaders? Consider using your high school students to lead your junior highers. Your junior highers will enjoy getting to know people who have recently been where they are, and your senior highers will gain valuable ministry and leadership experience.

Share these historical (and sometimes hysterical) pictures with junior highers and middle schoolers. Then send the kids out on a mission to find items from that era (or modern items that look similar) so they can decorate a room to look like a 100-year-old church sanctuary. This is a good activity to involve senior citizens in—have them help junior highers track down old items. Send one team of junior highers to gather information about what kind of music might've been a part of an old church service. They can find this information at a library in a book about hymnology.

When the group has collected all the supplies and information it can, have the kids decorate a room to look the way it might've in the "old days." Invite kids to dress as citizens of that historical time and attend a worship service to celebrate their heritage of faith.

During the worship service, have kids sing some of the old hymns and complete the following sentences.
- Our history of faith is important because...
- I'm who I am today because...
- One thing I'm thankful for about the Christians who've gone before is ...

Have someone read aloud Deuteronomy 32:7. Ask: **What questions would** you like to ask Christians who lived 100 years ago? How about 200 years ago? What issues do you think they dealt with that are similar to today's issues? What issues are different? How can we learn from the people who've gone before us to better live our lives of faith?

Scriptures for Deeper Study: Isaiah 41:1-4; Daniel 4:34.

Been There, Done That

Focus of the Fun: Junior highers and middle schoolers will visit a variety of sites in the community and photograph their experiences, then create a scrapbook of their adventures and discuss faith as an adventure.

Supplies: Instant-print cameras, scrapbooks, markers, tape, and Bibles.

Form groups of six to eight and give each group a loaded instant-print camera (and extra film if they'll have enough time to use more than one roll). Then say: **The object of this activity is to do as many fun and different things as a group as possible in the time allowed, and to capture your adventures on film for the whole group to enjoy. To do this, you'll first have to decide where you'll go and in what order you'll do the activities. Have someone in the group—or better yet, someone outside of the group—take the picture at each location. Then bring your pictures back in two hours** (or another time as determined by your schedule). Send the groups out on their adventures.

When kids return, give each group an empty scrapbook (or a sheet of poster board), tape, and markers, and have them write captions for their pictures.

When the scrapbooks are finished, have groups present them to the whole group and describe their experiences.

Then have someone read aloud Romans 5:1-2 and Proverbs 3:5. Ask: **How is faith like a big adventure? What elements of today's adventure could you apply to the adventure of faith? What unexpected things happened today in your adventures? What unexpected things have happened in your adventures of faith?**

Have kids look at the pictures they took and create a faith-related caption for each one. For example, a picture of kids having fun on a playground might have a caption that reads: "A life of faith is full of fun." Have kids share their captions with the whole group. Save your adventure scrapbooks and have kids look at them in a year or two and think about how far they've come in their faith adventures.

Scriptures for Deeper Study: Psalm 118:8; Ephesians 2:8; and Genesis 6:9–8:19.

Fields of Dreams

Focus of the Fun: Group members will learn to enjoy God's creation as they clean up a community park then play outdoor games.

Supplies: Trash bags, gloves, rakes, shovels, game equipment, snacks, and Bibles.

Young-Teenager Tip: Did you know that 84 percent of girls ages 8 to 17 are very concerned about kidnapping? (*100% American* by Daniel Evan Weiss)

Have kids gather outdoor maintenance supplies, such as rakes, trash bags, gloves, and shovels. Then (with permission from local officials if necessary), send kids out with adult sponsors to clean and beautify a park or field in your community. Depending on your location, kids may need such items as soap and scrub brushes (to clean graffiti) or large boxes (for trash that might tear plastic bags).

This project works best if kids have to work for a few hours at cleaning the park. While kids are cleaning, collect supplies for one of their favorite outdoor games (such as softball, volleyball, soccer, or disc golf) and snack foods. When kids have finished with their cleaning project (or have run out of time), have them sit in a circle to debrief the experience.

Ask: **What was it like to work on this project? How did your work help to restore God's beauty to the community?**

Have someone read aloud Genesis 1:26-31. Ask: **What's a Christian's responsibility to care for the world? How can we help keep God's earth beautiful? Is it possible to go "too far" in cleaning up the earth? Why or why not? How can we inspire other people to care for the earth?**

Celebrate and enjoy God's creation by playing some outdoor games and enjoying snacks together.

Scriptures for Deeper Study: Isaiah 6:3; 1 Corinthians 10:26; and Genesis 1:1.

Food for Everyone

Focus of the Fun: Kids will cook and deliver meals to church members and talk about what it means to be given a free gift.

Supplies: Cooking supplies, variety of foods, paper plates, plastic wrap, church directories, and Bibles.

Before this event, have kids help you determine a menu they'd like to prepare and serve to church members. Then have volunteers shop for the food and bring it to the church to prepare. A good lunch menu might include a sandwich (with individual condiment containers), potato chips, fresh vegetables, and cookies.

When kids arrive, form groups to prepare the various elements of the meal (one group for the main dish, one for the side dish, one for dessert, and so on). Then help kids to combine the elements into portable meals (use sturdy paper plates covered with plastic wrap).

Without notifying the people you're taking the meals to, send kids out to deliver them as a way of saying "thanks" for being faithful members of the church (or for helping with youth group events, or just for fun, or for any other reason). Kids will need to deliver enough meals to each house so all family members can enjoy one.

After the deliveries, meet with the kids back at the church. Ask: **What was it like to give something to someone when they weren't expecting it? How** did people respond to your free gift? How is the gift you gave these people like the gift God gave us in Jesus? How is your gift unlike God's gift?

Have a volunteer read aloud or quote from memory John 3:16. Ask: **How is God's gift like a wonderful surprise? The people we gave gifts to today may have deserved a gift for their goodness, but we didn't deserve God's gift of Jesus. How does that make you feel? What are ways we can show our gratitude to God for sending us the unexpected gift of Christ?**

Scriptures for Deeper Study: Matthew 7:11-12; Galatians 4:1-7.

Inquiring Minds

Focus of the Fun: Kids will do "field research" on a topic in three different places, then explore the truth that God is three in one.

Supplies: Three pencils, three pads of paper, and three Bibles.

Think of a subject that kids could study in three different, fun places. For example, if kids "research" the subject of fish, they could go to a sporting-goods store (fishing), a fish market, and an aquarium. If kids research the subject of music, they could go to a store that sells instruments and song books, a record store, and a radio station. Some other subjects they might study are painting, computers, food, space, law, sports, or dancing.

When kids arrive for the activity, have them form three groups. Say: **We are going to find out as much information as we can about** (name the subject). **Each group will go to a different place to find out about our topic.** Assign each group a leader and a place to study the subject. Give each group a pencil and pad of paper. Give the groups three or four hours to visit their places, ask questions of the experts in that place, make their own observations, and then write a report on what they learned.

Young-Teenager Tip: Sometimes including both junior and senior highers in an event can be a positive thing. But before doing this, consider your senior highers—if they'd likely look down on or belittle the junior highers instead of enjoy the opportunity to show them what it's like to be in the "older" group, you're better off keeping the groups separated.

When all three groups return to the church, have them read their reports to one another. Ask: **What is the perspective that each report had on our subject? How do the three different perspectives on the same topic relate to one another?**

Have each group read Galatians 4:4-6. Ask: **How might today's project be similar to the idea of God as three in one: Father, Son, and Holy Spirit? What's hard for you to understand about God as three in one? What can you learn from today's project to help you understand the idea that God is three in one?**

Scriptures for Deeper Study: Matthew 28:19; John 14:26; 2 Corinthians 13:14.

Movie of the Week

Focus of the Fun: Kids will create and star in a videotaped production depicting how their week has gone, then discuss how faith played a part in their lives during the week.

Supplies: Video cameras, blank videotapes, a VCR and monitor, and Bibles.

Form groups of no more than five and have them spend 10 or more minutes talking about the significant events of the past week. Then give each group a video camera and have them create a zany or serious movie depicting their past week. If you have a lot of groups and only a few cameras, have groups take turns using the cameras.

Young-Teenager Tip:
Did you know that 31 percent of kids ages 8 to 17 have no brothers? (*100% American* by Daniel Evan Weiss)

Encourage kids to have fun with their "movie of the week" productions and require each person to be involved in the production in some way. Some kids might choose to be actors while others hold props or run the camera. Have kids include at least one "scene" from each group member's week in their production.

When the videos are done, have groups play them for the rest of the group to enjoy. Then form new groups and have them discuss the following questions: **What was it like to relive the past week? What did you like about it? What didn't you like about it? What stands out about the videos we've seen? What do they tell us about the kind of week we've had? How could the week have gone better?**

Have someone read aloud Psalm 145:18. Ask: **When in the events of the past week did you call on God? How did God fit in the past week? How might your relationship with God have been better this past week? How can we live each week in close relationship with God? What might change in our lives if we spent more time with God?**

Save the videotapes and repeat this activity periodically to help kids think about God's role in their lives.

Scriptures for Deeper Study: James 4:8; Hebrews 4:16; John 14:6.

Nesting

Focus of the Fun: Kids will make a giant nest and discuss the home God is preparing for them in heaven.

Supplies: One Bible. (Optional: rakes and work gloves.)

This project works best in the fall. Go to a nearby park or a church member's home that has many trees, a place where there will be lots of fallen branches and leaves. You may want to travel to a nearby camping or picnic grounds. Find a clearing. Have kids build a nest, large enough to fit everyone in the group, by gathering branches and laying them next to and on top of one another to form a floor and then the sides. Fill the spaces with mud or wet sand to help it stay together. When the kids have finished the structure of the nest, have them line the inside with leaves.

When the group has finished constructing the nest, have them sit in it. Say: **Birds make nests for their homes. How would you like to live in this home? What makes a house a home? What are some things that make a house not feel like a home?**

Read John 14:1-4. Ask: **How do you feel knowing that God is building a home for you? What kind of preparations do you think God is making for our arrival? What aspects of home do you expect to find in heaven? What does it mean to have God as a heavenly Father of our home in heaven? How do you feel knowing that Jesus will come back to take you to that home?**

Scripture for Deeper Study: Matthew 8:20.

No Junk Here

Focus of the Fun: Junior highers will collect junk items from various homes and piece them together to form a statue representing the value God gives each person.

Supplies: Duct tape, nails, hammers, and Bibles. (Optional: scrap lumber and a camera.)

Form teams of no more than four. Say: **The object of this activity is to collect the most worthless junk you can find and bring it back to our meeting place. You must get the junk from people's homes and must ask for it by saying you're looking for worthless items.**

Send kids out on their journey. While they're gone, collect supplies such as duct tape, hammers, and nails for kids to use when they return. Any scrap pieces of wood will also help with the project.

When kids return, have volunteers share their stories of what it was like to ask people for worthless junk. Then have teams present their "goodies." When the items have been described, ask: **When you're feeling down, which of these items do you feel like? Explain. What kinds of things make us feel worthless or like junk?**

Have groups then use the duct tape, hammers, and nails to connect the worthless items into a symbol of great value (allow the kids to determine together what their symbol might be). After the junk has become a symbol of value, have someone read aloud Ephesians 2:1-4. Ask the following questions and have partners discuss them before sharing their insights with the whole group.

Ask: **What does this passage say about our value to God? How is God's grace a measure of his love for us? How is the way we gave value to this junk like the way God gives us value?**

If you brought a camera, have someone photograph the junk sculpture. Place the photograph in a prominent place in your meeting room as a reminder of how God values us even when we don't deserve it.

Scriptures for Deeper Study: Psalm 8; John 3:16; 1 John 3:1.

Puppet Stage

Focus of the Fun: Kids will work together to design and build a puppet stage for use by the children in the church, and then explore the childlike qualities Jesus wants us to have.

Supplies: PVC pipe or 2×4's, nails, hammers, curtain rods, curtain material, and Bibles.

Have kids gather the materials in a large workroom. Then help kids design a workable plan for building a puppet stage for use by the children in the church. The simplest design would include a frame for a curtain (about three feet high). Kids may want to be more inventive in their puppet-stage design. Work with kids to be sure you have the proper supplies before they begin construction on the stage.

(Note: If you have a large group and too many kids to work on the stage, have the rest collect old socks and other cloth materials to create hand puppets for the children.)

Young-Teenager Tip: The three most important traits a junior high worker needs to have are patience, patience, and patience. Your junior highers cover a wide range of maturity levels and are just as confused being themselves as you are trying to figure them out. Be patient. Watch and learn as your kids struggle through early adolescence and be ready to guide them when they make a wrong turn.

During a work break, have kids form groups of no more than four to read and discuss Matthew 18:1-6. Ask: **What does this passage tell us about children? How can we be more like children in our own lives? What's the difference between being childlike and childish? What positive childlike qualities do you see in the people around you? What qualities would you like to develop?**

When the puppet stage is complete, have kids work on a puppet show to share with the kids when they present the stage as a gift to them.

Scriptures for Deeper Study: Matthew 19:13-14; 21:14-16; Proverbs 17:6.

Race Cars

Focus of the Fun: Kids will race cars that they build out of scavenged materials and compare the Christian life to a race.

Supplies: Photocopies of the "Spare Parts" handout (p. 50); chalk; a roll of crepe paper (any color); two chairs of the same size; a whistle; first-aid supplies like adhesive bandages, antiseptic wipes, and first-aid cream (in case of spills, scrapes, and scratches); and Bibles.

Say: **Today we are going to build and race homemade race cars.** Form teams of no more than four. Give each foursome a copy of the "Spare Parts" handout. Say: **Your team has exactly four hours to build a race car from any materials on the "Spare Parts" list. You must also gather your materials in those four hours! Your car must be capable of racing across the church parking lot with one person from your team on board.** Clearly designate the time the race will begin and the penalty for being late to the starting line (for example, late teams start 10 feet behind punctual teams).

Near the time that the race will begin, draw a chalk line at one end of the parking lot and write "START" underneath the line. Then set up the finish line at the other end of the parking lot by placing two chairs on either side of the finishing point and tying crepe paper from one chair to the other.

When the groups arrive with their vehicles, line up the cars at the starting line. Say: **When I blow the whistle, the race will begin. Gentlemen and ladies, start your engines!** When everyone looks ready, blow the whistle. The first vehicle across the finish line wins. Run as many races as you like.

Afterward, gather the group together and ask: **How did you prepare to participate in this race? What was it like to put forth so much effort to win this race?**

Have foursomes meet around their vehicles and read 1 Corinthians 9:24-27, with each group member reading one verse. Ask the foursomes to discuss the question: **How was preparing for our race today like the verses we just read?** Have each foursome share with the rest of the group one answer to that question.

Scriptures for Deeper Study: 2 Timothy 4:7-8; Hebrews 12:1-3.

Rest Stopped

Focus of the Fun: Kids will serve refreshments all night to travelers at a rest stop to experience doing good even when they're tired.

Supplies: A coffee pot for heating water, extension cords, pitchers to hold hot water, packets of hot chocolate, tea bags, instant coffee, a pitcher of lemonade, cookies, hot-drink cups, cold-drink cups, paper napkins, plastic stirrers, an 8-foot long table, and Bibles. Kids will need to bring their own sleeping bags, pillows, toothbrushes, and toothpaste. (Optional: tents.)

Before beginning this project, scout out a rest stop where the group can stay overnight. Make sure it has an area to set up a refreshment table and

 (continued on page 51)

Spare Parts

- **Wheels**

- **Objects with wheels (For example, roller skates, skateboards, toys. Any object you use must become part of a larger vehicle—no fair having somebody roller skate or skateboard in the race and calling that person a race car!)**

- **Cans**

- **String or twine**

- **Wire**

- **Cloth**

- **Wood**

- **Boxes**

- **Construction tools (hammers, saws, nails, and so on)**

an area where the group can camp out. Call the state transportation department to obtain permission to stay overnight at that spot.

Say: **We're going to stay overnight at a rest stop to serve refreshments to travelers.** Have kids help gather the above supplies by shopping for them or gathering what they have at home to contribute to the project.

Upon arrival at the rest stop, have kids set up the refreshment table with the coffee pot (and start heating water), hot-water pitchers, packets for hot drinks (hot chocolate, tea, instant coffee), and cookies. Also have kids set up a camping area (either tenting or sleeping out under the stars) near the refreshment table before it gets dark.

Have kids assign themselves to shifts (for example, one team of kids could take the 10 to midnight shift) during which they will offer refreshments to travelers. Kids may (but probably won't) sleep when it is not their shift.

In the morning, have kids participate in a morning devotion about how it feels to encourage weary people on the road. Have the group read Galatians 6:9. Then ask: **What was it like to serve others when you were so tired? How was our overnight activity a reflection of the theme of Galatians 6:9?**

Scriptures for Deeper Study: Isaiah 40:28-31; 2 Thessalonians 3:13.

Skywriting

Focus of the Fun: Kids will sponge-paint encouraging messages and attach them to the ceilings of the people they wish to encourage.

Supplies: One Bible per student, one 20×30-inch piece of light blue construction paper for every two kids (you can find paper this large at an art store; look under "Artists' Materials—Retail" in your Yellow Pages), white tempera paint, two shallow bowls or dishes for the paint, one sponge per person, and masking tape. (If you use powdered tempera paint, mix it with water before beginning the activity.)

Pour the prepared paint into the shallow bowls or dishes. Place all of the supplies on a table.

Have the group read 1 Thessalonians 5:11 in unison. Ask: **What is one way you have fulfilled this Scripture in the past week? What are some ways we can encourage others on a daily basis?**

Say: **Today we're going to practice building up others by "skywriting" encouraging messages to people we care about.** Have kids form pairs. Tell pairs to think of someone they would like to encourage and an encouraging message they can write to that person. They can choose to encourage friends, a sick person in a hospital, a pastor at church, a family member, a favorite teacher, or anyone else. Encouraging messages could be "We're praying for you," a line from a special song, or a verse from the Bible.

Give each pair a piece of light blue construction paper. Have pairs create their encouraging message on the paper using the sponges as writing utensils. Sponges can be used in one of two ways:

1. Kids can dip the corner of the sponge in the paint and drag it like a brush to form letters. This option looks like skywriting.

2. Kids can cut their two sponges according to the pattern provided (see diagram on page 52). With the cut pieces, they can form all letters in the alphabet by

choosing the appropriate pieces (for example, two long, straight pieces and one short, straight piece can form an A). Then they can dip one side of each sponge piece into the paint, position the sponge on the paper, and gently push to apply the paint to the paper. This procedure makes the letters look like clouds.

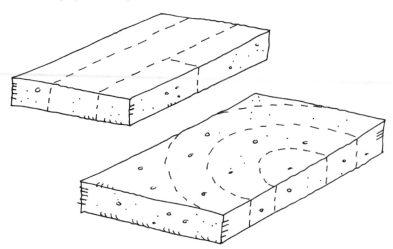

Young-Teenager Tip:

Do you ever notice how your junior high students can say the most negative remarks about your appearance, your mannerisms, and who you are as a person? These negative remarks expressed to adults are often a junior higher's way of separating themselves from the adults around them. Kids want to express their own identity as people with different opinions. When you can hear and accept (without believing) their negative comments and avoid striking back, many junior highers take that as a sign that you're accepting them as individuals. (*The Changing Family Life Cycle* by Betty Carter and Monica McGoldrick)

While the paint is drying, ask: **What were you thinking as you were "skywriting" encouraging messages for someone important to you? What made you think that? How would you feel if you received one of these messages? What do you think it will be like for the people you have chosen to encourage when they receive your "skywritten" message?**

When the paint is dry, hop into the church van or into a couple of cars driven by adults to have kids deliver their messages to the intended "encouragees." If at all possible, deliveries should happen when the recipient is not present. Have kids tape the messages to the ceiling of their friends' bedrooms, the pastor's study, or a hospital room.

Variations:

1. You can also use this project to promote group events. Have students create an ad for an upcoming event and tape it to the ceiling of the meeting room. Let kids discover it in their own time and share their discovery with their friends.

2. Fly a message on a kite for passersby to see. Or have a bunch of kids bring kites and write one word per kite, forming an encouraging sentence. Have the kids fly their kites in the right order and at the same time.

3. Get permission from your city (call City Hall) to place a banner across a street. Cut an old sheet in half, sew the short end of one half to the short end of the other half and paint an encouraging message on the banner in tempera paints. Make holes in the four corners of the combined sheets, gather four ropes, and tie one end of each rope through each hole. Attach the other end of the ropes to telephone poles.

Scriptures for Deeper Study: Psalm 10:17; Hebrews 3:13; Hebrews 10:25.

Focus of the Fun: Kids will use their talents to help others by performing in a street show.

Supplies: One Bible for every two students, an easel, one piece of poster board per act, colorful markers, and a hat. (Optional: a megaphone.)

Tell kids to arrive for this event with a special act they can do on the street without a sound system or electricity. For example, someone could play a trumpet piece, a few kids could develop a skit, or a pair of kids could create a juggling act. Determine a street corner downtown where kids can perform their acts one at a time. Call City Hall to determine whether you need permission to use that street corner for the afternoon. Also call nearby businesses to obtain their permission to occupy the area in front of their property for that afternoon.

Ask: **What is one time when you used a special talent you have to help someone else? How did that person respond? How did you feel when you helped that person by using your special gift?** Form pairs. Have pairs read Romans 12:6-8 with one person reading the passage and the other person creating a one-sentence summary of the passage. Have each pair share their summary with the whole group.

Say: **Today each of you has come prepared to perform an act in a street show. We will leave out a hat to collect change people wish to donate to us, and we'll give that money to someone who could use our help. Who do you want to help by using our talents in this street show?** Have kids brainstorm people or groups they can help, such as a favorite charity or a missionary family.

Young-Teenager Tip: Did you know that junior highers are prone to fatigue because their bodies concentrate so much energy on growing? Educator Samuel Campbell says, "Students who are growing rapidly have a low tolerance for fatigue . . . Fatigue has a dilatory effect on learning and conspires with fast physical growth to affect attention span so students really can't sit still for long periods of time." Overcome the fatigue hurdle by engaging junior highers actively in learning processes and mixing up meetings to keep their attention. (Samuel H. Campbell, "How Do We Meet the Needs of Early Adolescents?" The Education Digest)

Have kids create signs for their acts using the markers and poster board. For example, if a student will play his tuba, he could create a sign that says, "Tom and His Tremendous Tuba!" While kids are drawing their signs, list the order in which the kids will perform, varying the types of acts so that you don't have all the instrumental numbers in sequence, and so on. When kids have finished their signs, put the signs in the order you have listed.

Transport kids, their props and instruments, the signs, the easel, and the hat to the street corner you have chosen. Set up the easel, placing all the signs on it, and set the hat out so passersby can put money into it if they choose. Then have kids do their acts in the order you have determined.

When the kids have completed their acts, return to the church. Have kids be responsible for delivering or mailing the money they raised to the person or organization they chose.

Scripture for Deeper Study: 1 John 3:16-18.

Toll Kiss

Focus of the Fun: Kids will build a tollbooth to use in motivating Sunday school classes to encourage one another.

Supplies: One bag of Hershey's Kisses per student (tell each student to bring one bag to the activity), one large furniture or refrigerator box, scissors, black felt-tip markers, duct tape, index cards (six per student), transparent tape, a chair, and one Bible per student.

Before doing this project, explain the project to a teacher of one of the Sunday school classes and arrange to have the "tollbooth" set up at the entrance to that class.

When kids arrive for the project, say: **We are going to construct a toll-booth for** (the Sunday school class you've chosen). **Everyone who comes to Sunday school tomorrow will have to pay a toll of kindness to get into their room.**

Have the kids create a tollbooth structure by cutting one of the wider sides out of the refrigerator box. The box should stand upright with the bottom flaps on the outside. On the other wide side of the box, cut out a window at a level where a student sitting in a chair can see out (approximately 3 feet from the bottom of the tollbooth). Leave at least 5 inches around the edges of the window. When the structure is completed, tell kids to write "Tollbooth" across the top of the tollbooth window with marker and "Toll: A Kiss of Kindness" below the window.

Have kids make "coins" out of the Hershey's Kisses by taking six index cards, cutting each card into a circle with a 3-inch diameter, and covering each circle completely with kisses. Kids can use the inside circle of the roll of duct tape as a pattern for the circles. Have kids tape kisses to the cards using loops of transparent tape, sticky side out, and sticking the loop to the flat side of the Hershey's Kiss and then to the circle. Have each person tape three "coins" to the tollbooth using a loop of duct tape, sticky side out, to fasten the card to the refrigerator box. Have kids leave the rest of their "coins" inside the tollbooth for the next day.

Ask: **What is a kind word someone has said to you that you have never forgotten? How did it make you feel? How do you feel remembering it now?**

Have the group read Ephesians 4:32 in unison. Ask: **What are some ways we can put this verse into action? Tomorrow, when people come to Sunday school, they will receive two "coins" of Hershey's Kisses, give them to two different people, and say something kind to each person. What kinds of things can we encourage people to say that fulfill Ephesians 4:32?**

Set up the completed tollbooth at the entrance to the chosen Sunday school room, securing the bottom flaps to the floor outside the box with duct tape. At the next youth group meeting or Sunday school class, have the kids who built the tollbooth arrive early. Have the group take turns staffing it. Tell them to instruct each person who enters to take two "coins" of Hershey's Kisses, give them to two different people, and say something kind to each person in accordance with Ephesians 4:32. Everyone should give two "coins" and receive two "coins."

Scriptures for Deeper Study: Galatians 5:22-23: 1 Thessalonians 5:15: 2 Timothy 2:24.

Visions of Heaven

Focus of the Fun: Kids will create a parking lot-size chalk mural depicting heaven.

Supplies: Sidewalk chalk, ladder, camera, and Bibles.

Before this activity, have kids read Revelation 21:1-4 and discuss in trios what they think heaven will be like. Refer kids to the rest of Revelation 21 for inspiration for their discussions.

Have kids discuss such topics as:
- **What will be unique about heaven?**
- **How will we live each day in heaven?**
- **What feeling will people have in heaven?**
- **What will heaven look like?**

Allow 10 minutes for discussion, then take kids outside and have them take turns climbing a tall ladder to look down in your church parking lot (or another concrete or blacktop surface near the church).

Then divide the parking lot area into equal sections (one for each team of no more than three) and have kids transfer their ideas of what heaven might be like into chalk-art pictures to fill the parking lot.

During their work, encourage kids to get a bird's-eye view from atop the ladder or the church building (if it's OK with the property committee). Then, when the sections are complete, have kids each take a turn looking down on "heaven." Take a photograph of the artwork alone, and with the kids standing near their own designs.

Young-Teenager Tip: For up-to-date information on the latest video games your junior highers are playing, read PlayRight. It addresses the adult audience with facts about the newest games and about the industry in general. To subscribe, write or call PlayRight, P.O. Box 5830, San Mateo, CA 94402, 1-800-337-PLAY.

Scriptures for Deeper Study: Isaiah 66:1; Matthew 16:19; 2 Peter 3:13.

Water Armor

Focus of the Fun: Kids will create armor and engage in water-balloon warfare to illustrate the spiritual armor described in Ephesians 6:10-18.

Supplies: Two Bibles, two bags of water balloons, water, and two large garbage cans.

Form two teams. Have each team read Ephesians 6:10-18 and identify the six pieces of armor and their purposes. Say: **You have two hours to develop your own team armor that will guard you against water-balloon warfare. For example, you could use shower caps as helmets or umbrellas as shields. Your team must develop a piece of armor to correspond with each piece in the Ephesians passage. All team members must wear a suit of armor.**

Send out teams with drivers to gather the supplies they need to create their armor. While the teams are creating their armor, fill the water balloons and place an equal amount of balloons in each garbage can. Place one garbage can at each end of your church parking lot.

When teams are ready for war, assign each team a garbage can as their arsenal of water balloons. Give the group half an hour to engage in water warfare, and then have all team members remove their armor. Judge to see which team is drier than the other; that team wins.

Variations:
● Make a rule that all team members must travel in a connected group by interlocking their arms or tying a rope around the whole group.
● Have kids walk backward and throw the water balloons over their shoulders or through their legs.
● Turn this into a Capture the Flag game by dividing the playing area in half, having each team place a handkerchief in a designated area, and having the teams try to retrieve each other's flag. Kids who tag an opponent with a water balloon get three additional free water-balloon shots 10 feet away from the opponent. Then the opponent gets a free walk back to his or her side.

Scriptures for Deeper Study: Romans 13:12; 2 Corinthians 10:3-5; 1 Thessalonians 5:8.

Window Dressing

Focus of the Fun: Kids will make a window display to promote a church event and discuss communicating the Good News.

Supplies: "Window Display Evaluation Form" handouts, pencils, newsprint, paints, and masking tape.

Use this project to help kids learn about communicating a message that is important to them.

Before the project, determine a church or youth event you would like the kids to advertise (for example, an upcoming church camp or a holiday concert by the choir).

Make enough copies of the "Window Display Evaluation Form" handout on page 58 for every three kids to have one.

Say: **We are going to create a window display, like those you see at the mall, to advertise** (the upcoming church event). Transport the group to a local mall. When you arrive, have the group form trios. Give each trio a copy of the "Window Display Evaluation Form" and a pencil. Tell the trios to look at the window displays and respond to the questions on the form. Have them meet back at the vehicles in one hour.

When the kids return, transport them to the church. Have each trio share its responses to the "Window Display Evaluation Form" questions with the rest of the group. Based on their evaluations of the window displays the group saw, have the group design the window display for the event they'll be promoting.

Tape a sheet of newsprint to the wall. Have the group list all the details about the event they want to communicate to the congregation and write down the details on the newsprint.

Then have the group design a window display that would serve as an advertisement, making sure it addresses all the necessary details. The group will have to determine a space to set up the display (for example, outside the church doors), collect props (from their own closets, borrowing from friends, or buying from a thrift store), and practice setting up the display. They can obtain real mannequins on loan or rented from a retail supply center. The kids may also paint signs on newsprint with details that would not readily be communicated solely through the display (such as the cost of the event, the date, the time, and the place).

For example, if you were advertising an upcoming church picnic, you might have kids set up a picnic site outside the doors of the church. You could have them gather seven mannequins, a barbecue, a picnic table, some lawn chairs, a blanket, paper plates, a volleyball net, and other items you would find at a picnic. Then kids could set up the items accordingly: one mannequin set up to "flip" burgers; four mannequins "playing" volleyball; and a pair of mannequins sitting on the blanket holding a sign painted with "All-Church Picnic, July 3, 12:30 p.m."

When kids have gathered and created all of their props, have them set up their window display and make any needed adjustments. Then tell them to arrive before church on Sunday to make any final adjustments and to watch people's reactions to the display.

For discussion, ask: **How did we communicate a message to the people at church about the event? What do you think helped them understand what we were trying to say? How did you feel as people walked by and noticed our display? How is communicating as a window display like communicating about our faith?** Read Matthew 28:19-20. Ask: **How can we make our lives "window displays" for the gospel?**

Variation: Have kids be live mannequins within the window display. For example, in the church picnic window display, one junior higher could pretend to flip the hamburgers by holding a spatula in his or her hand with the arm bent at the elbow. The student can stand still or be a moving mannequin by bending slightly at the waist toward the barbecue, making a flipping motion with the spatula, and then straightening up again. Tell kids to make the movements robot-like by moving to their positions and bobbing up and down a bit as if snapping into place.

Scriptures for Deeper Study: Matthew 10:19-20; Colossians 1:28; 2 Timothy 4:2.

Window Display Evaluation Form

Directions: Use this list of questions for evaluating window displays at a mall.

● Which window displays do you like the best? Why?

● Which window displays do you like the least? Why?

● What are some of the messages communicated in the window displays?

● How are these messages communicated?

4 Long-Term Projects

Instant oatmeal, fast food, remote control channel surfing...our junior highers and middle schoolers are used to getting what they want NOW. Yet, sometimes investing now for a future gain can be a valuable experience.

Like the farmer who plants for a future harvest, you can use this chapter to involve your kids in projects that bring rewards over a period of time. All the projects here have their own biblical focus and, by their very nature, teach the value of patience and persistence and trust.

TIME FOCUS: A FEW DAYS, A FEW WEEKS, A FEW MONTHS, A YEAR!

NUMBER OF STUDENTS: VARIES, DEPENDING ON THE PROJECT.

Books on the Wall

Focus of the Fun: Kids will copy an entire book of the Bible onto a designated wall of their youth room until the wall is filled, and they will learn about the perseverance of the faithful.

Supplies: White paint, paintbrushes, permanent markers, and Bibles.

For this project to work, you'll need a large wall that kids can paint on somewhere in the church or youth room. Choose a wall that's flat (nontextured) if possible. To begin the project, have kids meet one afternoon to paint a coat of white paint on the chosen wall. Explain to kids that they'll be copying an entire book of the Bible onto the wall, using permanent markers, until they've filled the wall (or finished the book). This project works best when kids are also studying the book of the Bible they're copying.

Each week, have kids work in pairs to add more to the book of the Bible they're writing on the wall. Encourage kids to write small so there's plenty of room on the wall for the whole book (and perhaps another as well).

To involve all the members of your group at the same time, you'll need to assign each pair one section of the book and one portion of the wall. Have one member of each pair read the passage while the other writes the words on the wall. Remind kids to write small enough to fit the whole passage into their assigned portion of the wall. They can fill in any blank spaces later with illustrations.

If your group is so large that kids would get in each other's way while writing, involve kids sequentially. Assign two junior highers or middle schoolers to write each week, having one read the passage while the other writes the words onto the wall. A few others can add small illustrations or decorations to the completed portion of the wall to make it more decorative. Encourage kids to use illustrations that match with the theme of the book. Using lots of different-color markers also adds to the unique look of the wall.

As the wall is nearly filled (it may take a couple of books of the Bible, depending on which ones you use and how small kids write), meet to discuss the following questions: **What has it been like to work on this project for so long? What role has perseverance played in our project?**

Have someone read aloud James 1:12. Then ask: **How is this project an example of perseverance? In what life situations do we need to persevere?**

When the wall is done, unveil it for the whole church to enjoy. Kids will look at this project as a symbol of their own perseverance and as a symbol of their ability to work together. Consider doing this project every few years (using a new wall if possible).

Scriptures for Deeper Study: Hebrews 10:35-38; James 5:7-8; Revelation 13:9-10.

Business Cents

Focus of the Fun: Students will create a small business, determine the investment required, and discuss counting the cost of faith in Christ.

Supplies: Three Bibles. The rest of the supplies will be decided by the group.

Use this project in the summer.

Say: **We are going to create our own business. We need to form a board of directors to run the business, and we need investors. But first we need to determine what this business will be.**

Have kids brainstorm a business they would like to run for the summer. They could produce a product (for example, homemade greeting cards, advertisement flyers, or advertisement banners to post above a city street). Or they could have a service-oriented business (for example, tutoring elementary school kids in summer school, grocery shopping for people, or taking care of pets and plants while people are on vacation).

After kids have determined what kind of business to run, have the board of directors discuss how much money to invest, how much time to invest, how they will run the business, who will complete which tasks, and other necessary decisions. Have a couple of kids from the board of directors conduct research on the cost of materials to make their product or provide their service. Have other kids research the cost of advertising the product or service in local newspapers, newsletters, or even on the radio. Have these two research groups determine how much money the group will need to charge to make a profit on the business. Have a few more kids conduct market research by calling people to see if they would be interested in what the business will offer.

When everyone is ready, have the research teams report their information to the rest of the group. Then have the group vote on whether to go ahead with the project, committing to the money and time it will take to make the project a success. The group will need to decide at this time what they would like to do with the proceeds from the business. They can decide to raise funds for the youth department, or they can give their funds to a charitable organization they agree upon.

At the conclusion of this final meeting, ask: **What made you willing or unwilling to commit to this business venture? What else could we have done to make you more comfortable with going ahead with the project?**

Form three groups. Have Group 1 read Luke 14:25-27, Group 2 read Luke 14:28-30, and Group 3 read Luke 14:31-33. Tell the groups to develop a summary sentence for the passage that they read. Then have a spokesperson from each group share the group's summary sentence with the other groups.

Ask: **How is our business venture like this passage? How do we count the cost of committing our lives to Jesus? What did it take or what will it take for you to decide to follow him?**

Scriptures for Deeper Study: Philippians 3:7-9.

Carnation Experiment

Focus of the Fun: Kids will experiment with putting white carnations in different colors of water to illustrate that what we feed ourselves mentally and emotionally impacts who we become.

Supplies: White carnations, copies of the "Carnation Experiment Instructions" handout (p. 62), liquid food coloring (enough for each student to receive two different colors), and Bibles.

This project takes one week.

Say: **We're going to do a scientific experiment. We'll see if we can change the color of these white carnations.** Give each person one carnation, two colors of liquid food coloring, and a copy of the handout to take home. Read through the instructions with the group and ask if anyone has any questions about the experiment. Tell them to bring their carnations and recorded observations with them to next week's meeting.

When the group meets the next week, have kids compare their carnations. Ask: **What changes in the carnation did you observe during the week? How did these changes occur? What are ways that you "feed" yourselves emotionally and mentally? How can you tell when something you have taken in has "fed" you?**

Have the group read Philippians 4:8-9 aloud in unison. Ask: **What kinds of things meet the description in Philippians 4:8-9? What would happen if we fed only ourselves with these things?**

Say: **Let's do another experiment. Let's feed ourselves with these things this next week and share what we observe next week.**

(continued on page 63)

Carnation Experiment Instructions

Day One: Put carnation in a vase (or glass) full of clear water.

Day Two: In the morning, observe any changes in the carnation. Record your observations below. In the evening before you go to bed, replace the water in the vase with one-quarter inch of water and one-eighth inch food coloring (any color).

Day Three: In the morning, observe any changes in the carnation. Record your observations below. In the evening before you go to bed, replace the water in the vase with one-quarter inch of water and one-eighth inch of a different color of food coloring.

Day Four: In the morning observe any changes in the carnation. Record your observations below. If you wish, repeat the coloring process before you go to bed. If not, place the carnation in a vase full of clear water until the next meeting.

Day Five: Observe any changes in the carnation. Record your observations below.

Bring your carnation to our next meeting.

OBSERVATIONS

Day Two:

Day Three:

Day Four:

Day Five:

Variation: Tell some kids to slice the stem down the length of the carnation and place one half of the stem in a glass with one color and the other half in another glass with another color. Then have them observe the changes.

Scriptures for Deeper Study: 1 Corinthians 3:2; 1 Peter 2:2.

Doodle Doozy

Focus of the Fun: Group members will take turns adding their doodles to sheets of poster board as a way of opening up and encouraging one another.

Supplies: Sheets of poster board, markers, tape, and Bibles.

Give a sheet of poster board and a thin-line marker to two or three group members. Have these kids take the poster board home and draw or write on it during the week.

Tell kids to include illustrations and thoughts that will encourage other group members. For example, someone might write a general note to the rest of the group saying how much he or she appreciates them. Or someone might draw a picture of a heart with the names of group members in the middle. Explain that the object of the project isn't to show off as artists or writers, but to capture their personalities on the poster board and to encourage one another.

Each week, have someone new take one of the poster-board sheets home to add to the previous person's doodling. Continue passing the poster-board sheets around until they're completely filled (the more crowded they are, the better).

Note: Be sure to review the poster board for possible negative or inappropriate messages or illustrations. If you find some, you can cover them up with Liquid Paper or a dark marker.

When the poster-board sheets are filled, tape them to a wall in your youth room. Have kids read aloud Hebrews 10:25. Ask: **What are ways we've encouraged each other in this project? How can we continue to encourage one another?**

Keep the poster-board sheets up in the room as long as possible to remind kids of their support for one another.

Scriptures for Deeper Study: Proverbs 12:25; 16:24.

Young Teenagers' Little Instruction Books

Focus of the Fun: Kids will write a manuscript sharing messages about God and submit it to publishers.

Supplies: Paper, pencils, a computer with a word processing program or a typewriter, and one Bible per trio of students.

This project will take approximately three weeks.

When students gather for the first time to work on this project, have them form trios. Give each trio a Bible, and have the whole group read 1 Timothy 4:11-

13 aloud and in unison. Ask: **What does this passage say about sharing what we know about God?**

Say: **Each of you has important things to share about life and about your relationship with God. Today we are going to begin writing a book of "little instructions" that shares what we know about life and God.** Give each trio a small stack of paper and pencils and encourage kids to brainstorm as many little instructions as they can. For example, they may write, "A steady diet of Bible reading leads to a healthy soul." You may want to bring in H. Jackson Brown Jr.'s *Life's Little Instruction Book* to give them an example of what they will be creating. Challenge your whole group to develop 365 little instructions. Have each trio write down all of the little instructions they brainstorm.

You may want to spend another meeting brainstorming more little instructions, giving your kids time between sessions to think of some on their own.

When the group has reached the goal of 365 little instructions and written them all down on paper, form four groups. Have one group type the little instructions into the computer or on the typewriter. Have another group research publishers to whom you could send the manuscript. When the typing group has typed all of the little instructions into the computer or on paper, have a third group type a cover letter to send to each publisher. Have the fourth group oversee the copying and sending of the manuscript to each publisher.

Scriptures for Deeper Study: 1 Thessalonians 2:4; 2 Timothy 1:13-14; 3:14-15.

Launch Time

Focus of the Fun: Kids will launch a football over a large building and explore overcoming obstacles.

Supplies: A Nerf football, a ladder, and Bibles. The other supplies will be determined by the group.

This project has a one-week time limit. Determine an area where kids can launch the Nerf football over the church building or some other tall obstacle. Make sure it is a place where no one will be hurt by the Nerf ball when it lands.

Form teams of four. Hold the Nerf football in your hand and say: **Each group must develop a method of launching this football over the church building. You have one week to develop a way to overcome the obstacle of the church building and send the football to the other side of it. You can use anything you create as a team. You cannot buy a ready-made launcher of any type, and you cannot simply throw the football over the roof. Your money limit is $12 per group, with each person spending up to $3. You may want to practice launching another soft object so you can be sure your launcher will work next week.** Tell kids when and where to meet to launch the football.

When kids arrive during the next week, have them set up their launchers. Then allow groups to try to launch the football over the building. If kids are unsuccessful, allow them to make adjustments and try again until they can be successful. Have kids who are not launching use a ladder to fetch the football off the roof for those groups who are launching.

When every group has successfully launched the football, gather together in a group. Ask: **What did it take to overcome the obstacle of the church building? How did you prepare so you knew your launcher would work? What are some obstacles in your everyday life that you need to overcome? How do you overcome them? What do you learn from these obstacles that you encounter?**

Have every group read James 1:2-4 and summarize the passage in one sentence. Have the groups share their summary sentences with the larger group. Ask: **What does this passage say about meeting obstacles in our lives? What is one thing you have learned from encountering an obstacle in your life?**

Scriptures for Deeper Study: Romans 5:3-5.

Life-Size Gingerbread Person

Focus of the Fun: Kids will make a life-size gingerbread person to illustrate that they are the body of Christ.

Supplies: A recipe and ingredients for three batches of gingerbread dough (check your local library for a cookbook such as *Better Homes and Gardens New Cook Book*), access to a kitchen, and ready-made icing. You'll want decorative items such as chocolate chips, M&M's, marshmallows, raisins, and decorative sprinkles as well. You'll also need Bibles, and may want to bring a camera and film.

Your group can complete this project in two days. Tell everyone the goal of this project is to create a life-size gingerbread person.

On day one, make all three batches of cookie dough with all of your students helping. Assign each student an ingredient, and tell your students that they are responsible for making sure that their ingredient is put into each batch of cookie dough. While making the cookie dough, ask: **What part does each ingredient play in making the cookie dough taste right? What would happen if we forgot one or more of the ingredients—for example, molasses or baking soda? Which ingredients require the least amount for this recipe? What would happen if we forgot those ingredients?**

Ask a volunteer with clean hands to read 1 Corinthians 12:12-31 aloud to the group. Ask: **How is making cookie dough like belonging to the body of Christ as described in 1 Corinthians 12:12-31? What part of the body of Christ are you?** (Make sure each student answers this last question.)

Young-Teenager Tip: While you shouldn't spend every waking moment with your young teenagers, sometimes a surprise activity can do wonders for kids' days. Call kids together for a pick-up game of basketball or a walk in a local park. Choose an activity where kids simply have fun being together.

When you have finished making the cookie dough, refrigerate it overnight. Tell kids to return the next day to create your life-size gingerbread person.

On day two, preheat the oven to the appropriate temperature. Take one batch of dough out of the refrigerator. Have kids form a head and a body on two separate cookie sheets, making the body parts life-size using themselves as measures. The dough should be patted down to approximately one-quarter inch in thickness. Remember that the gingerbread will puff up and expand during baking, so take that into account when forming body parts. (For example, when creating the hands, make sure that the gingerbread is far enough apart so the two hands don't expand into one blob.)

Put those two cookie sheets into the oven, and then have kids use two more cookie sheets and more cookie dough to form hands and feet. When the first two cookie sheets are out of the oven, place the cookies on wax paper to cool. Then use the cookie sheets and more cookie dough to form two arms. Continue the process to form two thighs and two calves.

While the cookies are baking and cooling, have kids add food coloring to the icing to create several different colors of icing. (Be sure you leave some white icing, though).

When the cookies have cooled, have kids create a gingerbread person by placing the body cookies onto aluminum foil in the appropriate positions and "gluing" body cookies together with white icing. When the group has completed constructing the gingerbread person, allow them to decorate the person with the rest of the white icing, the colored icing, the candies, and the other decorative items.

When the gingerbread person is fully decorated, take a group picture with the kids and the gingerbread person.

Ask a volunteer to reread 1 Corinthians 12:12-31. Say: **Let's share how we see each other in the body of Christ. One by one we are going to take a piece of the gingerbread person and give it to someone else. As we do, we will share what we see as that person's important place in the body of Christ.** Have every person share once and every person receive a piece of cookie. Have kids wrap their cookie pieces in some aluminum foil and take them home for their dessert that night.

Scriptures for Deeper Study: Romans 12:4-8; Ephesians 1:22-23.

Lost and Found

Focus of the Fun: Kids will create a giant collage, search for hidden pictures, and explore how God searches until he finds us.

Supplies: Enough newsprint to cover one of your meeting-room walls, masking tape, a stack of old magazines, and one Bible per student.

The collage will take a week to create, but the search for hidden pictures may take a few weeks.

Before kids arrive to begin the project, measure the height and width of one of the walls of the youth group meeting room. Figure out how much newsprint will be necessary to cover that wall and provide enough pieces to do the job. Make sure that you have enough pieces for each student to have one. If you have fewer pieces of paper than students, cut the pieces of newsprint in half. If you have more pieces than students, plan to give some students two or more pieces of newsprint.

When kids arrive, say: **We are going to create a giant "Where's Waldo" type of search on this wall.** Give each student at least one piece of newsprint and make sure that all of the newsprint is given away so the whole wall will be covered. Also make available the stack of old magazines. Say: **Over this coming week, each of you will create a piece of our "Where's Waldo" wall. During the week, cover the piece of newsprint with magazine pictures from this stack of magazines, from old magazines you have at home, or by drawing your own pictures all over the paper if you wish. Be sure to use only appropriate pictures for the youth group room. If you're in doubt about a certain picture, leave it out. When you're done creating your piece of the wall, choose two pictures from it. On a separate sheet of paper, write one sentence that clearly describes each picture you have chosen—for example, "A little boy in a striped shirt sitting on his father's shoulders." For this project to work, the descriptions need to be really specific. Before next week's meeting, either drop off your two sentences to me or call me and tell them to me over the phone.**

When students have all called in their descriptions, type a list of the descriptions and make enough copies of the list for each student to have one.

At the next meeting, have students bring their newsprint and tape it onto the wall. Give everyone a copy of the list of things to find. Give kids time to look for all the items on the list. Award a prize—like a free ticket to the next big youth event—to the first person who can show the group where all of the pictures are.

At the end of the meeting, ask: **What is it like to look for all of these pictures? How do you feel when you find one, especially one that seems particularly difficult to find?** Have all of the students open their Bibles to Luke 15:1-7 and ask a volunteer to read the passage aloud while the rest follow along silently. Ask: **How is our activity like this parable Jesus told about the lost sheep? What does this passage mean to you? How can we be a part of Jesus' work of finding all of his lost sheep?**

Note: The students may not be able to find everything in one meeting. Allow the group to look again during other meetings until someone has found all of the items. Then award the prize!

Scriptures for Deeper Study: Luke 15:8-10,11-32.

Magic Show

Focus of the Fun: Kids will develop a magic show and contrast "magic" with the power of the Holy Spirit.

Supplies: One Bible for every two students. The rest of the supplies will be determined by the group.

Say: **We are going to create a magic show to share with other youth groups.** Have kids form pairs. Tell each pair to develop two magic tricks during the week. They can go to the library and look for books about magic tricks like *Bill Severn's Big Book of Close-Up Magic* by Bill Severn or *Shazam! Simple Science Magic* by Laurence B. White Jr. and Ray Broekel.

At the next meeting, have pairs perform their magic tricks for each other as a rehearsal for the magic show. Allow each pair to perform. Then have pairs read Acts 8:9-25. Ask: **What do you feel like when you can perform a magic trick, especially when no one can figure out how to do it? What do you think Simon felt like when he could perform magic tricks? What do you think he felt like when he saw Peter and John pray for others to receive the Holy Spirit? How did he feel after Peter and John responded to him? What does this passage have to say about the power of the Holy Spirit? What should our attitude be about the Holy Spirit?**

Schedule some performances of your magic show with other youth groups, for after-school child-care programs, or for a nursing home.

Scriptures for Deeper Study: John 15:26-27; 16:7-15; Acts 2:1-4; Romans 8:26-27.

Memento Ceiling

Focus of the Fun: Group members will collect and attach to the ceiling mementos from their youth group experiences.

Supplies: Bibles, a notebook, various items the kids collect, masking tape and nails or "cargo nets" of the type used to hold toys.

This project is actually a year-long activity for kids. While it doesn't take long to introduce and implement, it will provide lasting memories.

Open a meeting to introduce the project by having kids share their favorite memories from the past year. Then say: **Remembering our past is important as we look ahead to the future. So we're going to begin creating a lasting memory of our upcoming year.**

Have groups of no more than four read and discuss Psalm 77:11-12. Ask: **Why is it important to remember God's deeds? How can remembering the events that brought us to where we are help us grow in faith?**

Explain that kids will be collecting "memories" during the coming year and attaching them to the youth-room ceiling. For example, kids might collect a paper plate, a pine cone, and a empty box of graham crackers from a camping trip, or ticket stubs from a baseball game. Tell kids to collect items (not including food or other messy items) from each youth group event. Then have kids attach the items to the ceiling (use masking tape for the light items and nails for the heavier items).

You might want to simplify the attachment process by hanging a few cargo nets (or toy nets) across the ceiling, then place the items in the nets. Have kids write a description of each item (and what it represents) in a logbook that will be kept in the meeting room.

If you plan on keeping this project going more than one year, designate a section of the ceiling for each year. Kids who return to visit the room after graduating from your group will enjoy remembering the fun they had while in your group.

Scriptures for Deeper Study: Deuteronomy 5:15; Psalm 103:17; Exodus 3:15; Ecclesiastes 12:1-8.

Monstrous Mosaic

Focus of the Fun: Kids will create a large mosaic depicting a favorite Bible story.

Supplies: Sheet of plywood, paint, paintbrushes, pencils, glue, and Bibles. Kids will gather miscellaneous items appropriate for making a mosaic (such as buttons, rocks, rice, pasta). (Optional: camera and film.)

To do this activity, you'll need a large space where kids can work. When choosing where kids will work, keep in mind that the project may take a number of weeks to finish.

Have kids brainstorm which of their favorite Bible stories they'd like to illustrate in a mosaic. Suggest the following ideas: Noah's story (Genesis 6–8), the Israelites crossing the Red Sea (Exodus 14), Jonah and the big fish (Jonah), or the Sermon on the Mount (Matthew 5). Encourage kids to choose a story that translates well into a picture or scene.

When the kids have chosen their scene, form groups of no more than four to sketch illustrations that might be included in the scene. You may want to choose one of the ideas for the whole sheet of plywood or have each person add his or her own illustration to form a montage of scenes. Have kids paint the plywood a neutral color. After it dries, volunteers can use pencils to sketch their illustrations onto the board. It's best if the entire board is covered by illustrations (whether it's one scene or many).

With the illustrations penciled in, kids may begin to collect small items such as dried vegetables, rice, rocks, pasta, and other items to "color" their picture.

Young-Teenager Tip: According to the Gesell Institute of Human Development, a teenager's foremost interests are "making friends and having a good time." (*Your Ten- to Fourteen-Year-Old* by Louise Bates Ames, Frances L. Ilg, and Sidney M. Baker)

Periodically, have kids bring in their small items and glue them onto the mosaic. Help kids fill in the board completely, one item at a time. Explain that there are to be no "dumping everything on at once" shortcuts for the project. This will require kids to work together better and to learn patience. It will also yield a better finished product.

Over the course of the project, take photographs of the work in progress. Then celebrate the finished work by displaying it in the church along with the photographs. Kids and adults alike will enjoy seeing the fruit of their labor.

Debrief the project by asking kids how putting the mosaic together is like putting our lives together or figuring out our faith.

Variation: Tell kids that the finished mosaic must consist of items that haven't been artificially colored (they must remain their natural color). This will require kids to search harder to find items with the colors they need.

Scriptures for Deeper Study: Job; Romans 5:1-5.

The Never-Ending Sport

Focus of the Fun: Kids will learn about God's faithfulness as they participate in a sporting event that continues over a long period of time.

Supplies: Sports equipment, poster board, markers, tape, and Bibles.

Have kids select a favorite team sport that measures victory by a score (for example, volleyball, basketball, baseball, or soccer). Form two teams (teams can include more than the usual number required by a sport). Then have each team choose a team name.

Explain to kids that they're going to play a year-long version of the sport and keep track of the score to determine which team will treat the other to a party at the end of the year. Begin playing the sport and record the day's score on a large sheet of poster board.

Throughout the year, play the sport whenever possible. Keep adding the scores on your poster board until the final round of the game is played. Have the winning team treat the losers to a party. (The winning team will need to organize and collect food, music, and games for the party.) Be sure to report the winning score to your congregation for their amazement.

During the party, have kids read Genesis 9:12-17. Then ask: **What was it like to faithfully play our sport throughout the year? How is our faithfulness in this activity like God's faithfulness in this passage? What are other examples of God's faithfulness? Why is it important to remember God's faithfulness?**

Variation: To avoid unhealthy competition, you might have a few kids rotate from team to team each week so that everyone plays on each team throughout the course of the project. Then treat all teams to a party at the end of the year.

Scriptures for Deeper Study: 1 Chronicles 16:12; Ecclesiastes 12:1-8; Exodus 2:24; Luke 1:69-75.

Pennies, We've Got Pennies

Focus of the Fun: Junior highers and middle schoolers will collect 100,000 pennies and learn about how a little can go a long way.

Supplies: Large glass jars, paper, markers, tape, and Bibles.

Have kids research charitable organizations. Then have kids collect a bunch of large glass jars and use paper and markers to create labels for the jars indicating the charity they've chosen.

Have someone read aloud Luke 21:1-4. Then have trios discuss the following questions: **What was important about the two coins the widow contributed? In what other areas of life does a little bit mean a lot? What was more important, the amount given or the heart of the giver? Explain.**

Say: **We're going to see if we can collect 100,000 pennies—that's $1,000—to contribute to our charity. We'll ask people to give from the heart, but to give only pennies (which should be pretty easy to part with).**

Have kids brainstorm ways to collect pennies for their charity. Then have them choose a target date for collecting all 100,000 pennies. Help kids implement their various ideas and keep track of the growing funds.

Young-Teenager Tip:
"Encouragement + Challenge = Growth"

You'll need lots of jars for the pennies, so make collecting jars an ongoing part of the project. Kids will need a lot of encouragement because this activity may take a long time to complete. When they've finally collected 100,000 pennies, celebrate with a penny-rolling party and then deliver the pennies to your local bank for counting (and converting to lighter paper money).

As kids present the money to the charity, tell them to think about how they were able to collect the money, one penny at a time, and to remember that it's not the amount that's important in giving, it's the heart of the giver.

Scriptures for Deeper Study: Zechariah 7:9; Acts 20:35.

A Penny for Your . . .

Focus of the Fun: Kids will trade pennies for more valuable objects to explore making the most of what God gives them.

Supplies: One penny per student, Bibles, paper, pens, two sheets of newsprint, masking tape, and a marker.

This project takes one week.

Give each student a penny at one meeting. Say: **You have one week to turn this penny into anything you can. The idea is to improve upon the penny and get something you like better. The way you do this is by trading your penny with someone for something else, like a pencil. Then trade that object for something else. For example, trade the pencil for a pack of gum. You have all week, until our next meeting, to make trades with people you know. Remember, you are trading for keeps. Next week, bring what you end up with.**

When kids arrive at the next meeting, have kids show the objects they finally received and tell stories about how they ended up with those items.

Have kids form foursomes and give each foursome a Bible, a sheet of paper, and a pen. Tell each group to read Matthew 25:14-30 and then write two lists with the following headings, one on each side of the paper.

1) Our penny activity is like the passage because . . .

2) Our penny activity is different from the passage because . . .

While the groups are interacting, tape the two pieces of newsprint to the wall with masking tape, and label one piece "Similar" and the other "Different." After five minutes, have groups share one way they feel the activity was like the passage and one way it was different. Have each foursome share one of each and then allow any groups to add anything else they brainstormed that wasn't yet mentioned.

Ask: **What has God given you as a person that you could use to serve him? How will you use that talent this week? What results do you think you will experience from using your talents and abilities? How can you make the most of what God has given you as a person?**

Scriptures for Deeper Study: Luke 16:10-13; 19:11-27.

Satellite Gardens

Focus of the Fun: Kids will grow and maintain gardens as they learn about the importance of caring for each other and for the world.

Supplies: Gardening supplies, seeds, and Bibles.

Before this activity, you'll need to find enough garden sites for each group of four kids. Many congregation members (especially retired folks) have a small area of land in their yards that would serve well as a small garden.

Form teams of no more than four and assign each group to be caretakers of one of the garden plots. In the spring, after collecting gardening supplies from generous congregation members, send kids out to their sites to plant vegetable and/or flower gardens. Then, during the spring and summer, have kids care for the gardens by weeding them and watering as much as possible. Visit the sites yourself from time to time to check on kids' progress.

After the gardens have begun to grow, meet with kids to discuss what the experience has been like. Meet periodically after that to check on kids' feelings. Have kids read Genesis 2:15 and John 21:15-19 and discuss questions like: **How is this work an example of caring for God's world? How has your gardening experience gone so far? How is the way gardens grow like the way people grow? What impact has your care had on making the gardens grow? How is that like the impact we can have on caring for our world? caring for other people?**

You'll need a little help from the members of your congregation with "green thumbs" for trouble-shooting and determining when items are ready to pick. As vegetables are ready, have kids pick them and give them to the garden's owner. Or have them bring the food to the church to place on a giveaway table. At the end of the growing season, have kids report on the successes and failures of their gardening experiences.

Scriptures for Deeper Study: 1 Timothy 6:20-21; 1 Peter 5:1-4.

Time Capsules

Focus of the Fun: Kids will make personal time capsules and explore learning from the past.

Supplies: One mailing tube per person (available at a local post office or stationery store), paper, an assortment of colorful markers, masking tape, and Bibles.

Use this project to help kids understand how they can learn from their past and see how they have grown.

This project takes a week to put together, but the final result happens after one year.

At the end of one youth group meeting, say: **We are going to create time capsules for ourselves during the upcoming week. I am going to give each of you a mailing tube. During the week, fill the mailing tube with objects that are meaningful to you but that you won't need for the next** year. For example, you might want to put a special note from a friend, a shell or rock you collected on a trip, or anything else that brings back a special memory for you. Or you could create something that expresses where you are at this time in your life. For example, you could write a letter to yourself, write a poem, or make an audio tape in which you talk about your favorite song, your favorite TV show, and any events you are looking forward to within the next year. Fill your time capsule with at least five things and bring it back next week.

When kids return the next week, form groups of up to four students. Have kids share what they've put in their time capsules, and why those items are meaningful to them and express who they are at this point in their lives. Give each student a sheet of paper. Instruct students to use colorful markers to write their names on the paper and a message saying "Do Not Open Until (one year later)." Then have kids tape these messages to their mailing tubes with masking tape and tape their tubes shut.

Ask: **What do you think it will be like to open these time capsules in a year? Why are memories important to us? What do we learn from what we remember?**

Have kids in foursomes read Mark 6:30-52, with each student reading five or six verses of the passage. Ask: **What did the disciples in this passage need to learn from the feeding of the 5,000 that would have helped them when Jesus walked on water? What are some things from your past that have helped you deal with situations that happened later? What is one of your memories that has taught you something?**

When kids leave, tell them to "bury" their time capsules somewhere at home where they won't find them for awhile. For example, they may want to bury their time capsules under their beds, in the attic, in the garage, or in a seldom-used closet.

Put a note on your calendar to send postcards to your students after one year to remind them that they can open their time capsules.

Variation: Have kids "bury" their time capsules somewhere at church, such as in a supplies closet, in your office behind your desk or a bookshelf, or in a seldom-used room in the sanctuary. Put a note on your calendar to gather your group together again to "dig up" their time capsules. Ask: **What kinds of things are you remembering as you look at these objects? What do these objects have to say about your past and where you are now? What have you learned from this activity?**

Scriptures for Deeper Study: Deuteronomy 8:2-5; John 14:26.

Young-Teenager Tip: According to psychologists Emily B. Visher and John S. Visher, adolescents whose parents are divorced often switch residences, from living with mother to living with father or vice versa. Visher and Visher claim that teenagers "are concerned with identity issues and often choose to live with their other parent to experience that person more intimately than they have in their immediate past." (*Old Loyalties, New Ties: Therapeutic Strategies With Stepfamilies* by Emily Visher and John Visher)

Toothpick Masterpieces

Focus of the Fun: Kids will learn about perseverance and patience as they create sculptures out of toothpicks.

Supplies: Toothpicks, glue, tape, and Bibles.

For this project, allot a "toothpick time" in each group meeting for at least 10 weeks in a row. Explain that the object of this project is to create huge sculptures using only toothpicks, glue, and tape.

Form pairs and have kids brainstorm what they want to create out of the toothpicks. The bigger the idea, the better. For example, some might want to build a replica of your church, or a vehicle, or a large cross. Encourage kids to think big and let them know they'll have plenty of time to work on the project.

When pairs have finalized their plans, have them explain them to the rest of the class. Then give kids time to begin working on their toothpick creations. Be sure you're using a good, fast-drying wood glue so kids can see some accomplishment during the project. Kids may use tape to temporarily hold toothpicks together while the glue dries.

During one of the project times, call kids together for a brief Bible study. Have partners look up and read Ecclesiastes 7:8-9 and discuss the following questions: **How does this passage apply to our project? What emotions have you felt during this project? How are those similar to the feelings people have about other aspects of life? Why is patience important in everyday life? at school? with regard to your faith?**

When the projects are finally finished, have kids debrief the experience and tell what they learned because of it. Display the creations in the church sanctuary as a tribute to the role persistence can play in our lives.

Scriptures for Deeper Study: Psalm 19:11; James 5:7-8.

Youth Group Yearbook

Focus of the Fun: Kids will create a yearbook to help them reflect on their past year, the experiences they had, and the lessons they learned.

Supplies: One or two 35 mm cameras, black and white film, a computer with a word processing program or a typewriter, paper, glue sticks, tape, and Bibles.

This project can cover your whole youth group year, starting with summer activities and concluding the following spring, when kids can sign each other's yearbooks.

When you gather your group of students together, have each student read 1 Kings 11:41 silently. Ask: **Why do you think that everything Solomon did was recorded? What would it be like to read these books about his life as a king? What do you think you might learn from reading them? What do you learn from reflecting on things you have done in the past?**

Say: **We are going to create a youth group yearbook that will chronicle our events throughout the year, recording what we do and what we learn.** Form committees to be responsible for the various parts of the yearbook.

● Photography Committee—Responsible for photographing all youth group events using black and white film. This committee must keep track of which photos represent which events. They will also be in charge of assuring that everyone in the youth group is photographed and that at least one photograph of each person is in the yearbook.

● Writing Committee—Responsible for writing captions to accompany the photos as well as a few paragraphs summarizing each event and recording specific memories. For example, if you go on a ski trip during the winter, this committee would write a paragraph on what happened during the event, what they learned from Scripture-focused discussions, and some funny memories.

● Graphics Committee—Responsible for producing or procuring art for the yearbook. For example, students on this committee can draw pictures representing different activities or select graphics from a clip art book.

● Layout Committee—Responsible for organizing photos and copy on each page and preparing the final product for printing.

Throughout the year, hold Yearbook Committee meetings. Have the above committees work together to complete their responsibilities. For example, have the Photography Committee show the Writing Committee which photos go with which events and give suggestions for writing ideas.

Have the Layout Committee put the photos, writing, and graphics together into one final draft. This can be done in one of two ways:

I. On a Computer. Have the Layout Committee work on a computer with a word processing program. Aldus PageMaker is especially good for creating various publications and for inserting graphics. You may even consider scanning the photos into the document directly if you have access to a scanner. Kinko's Copies usually has computers with scanners that you can use in their stores for an hourly rental fee.

2. Cut, Paste, and Photocopy. Using the old cut-and-paste method, kids can lay out the design of each page manually. First, have kids sketch out how they want each page to look—where the photographs will fall and where the text copy will fall. Next, have committee members type up the text so it will fit into the space provided by the design. Kids may have to type the copy in different ways (for example, using narrow or wide margins) to get everything to fit onto the designed page. Or kids may want to use a photocopier with enlarging and reducing capabilities to make the typed text bigger or smaller until it fits in the space on the designed page. When they're ready, have the committee lay out each designed page of the yearbook on a sheet of paper with the actual photos, text copy, and graphics placed where they want them. Then have kids attach everything to the paper using a glue stick or transparent tape. This will create a final draft of each page so the actual yearbook can be printed.

In the spring, when you have a draft ready, bring your draft to a print shop such as Kinko's Copies. Have them print up the final product and put your yearbooks on sale. Have your whole youth group prepay for their yearbooks so you know how many to order from the print shop.

When kids receive their yearbooks, ask: **What is one thing in this yearbook that taught you something valuable in the past year? What will you do in the future because you have learned this lesson?** Allow kids to sign each other's yearbooks if they wish.

Young-Teenager Tip: According to the Gesell Institute of Human Development, as kids grow older, their individual differences in school capabilities become more noticeable. (*Your Ten- to Fourteen-Year-Old* by Louise Bates Ames, Frances L. Ilg, and Sidney M. Baker)

Variation: Call a yearbook company like Jostens and arrange to have the youth group yearbook professionally printed. Call their Small Book department at 1-800-248-9725 and inquire about pricing and procedures.

Scriptures for Deeper Study: Psalms 18:16-29; 40:1-3; James 4:13-17.

5 Grand-Ideas Projects

What's the biggest and most outrageous project you've ever done with your students? Believe it or not, the projects in this chapter are even bigger and more outrageous. Grand-Ideas Projects take more time and resources than other projects, but they are still possible. Want your kids to stretch beyond their normal boundaries? Try a "grand idea" and give your kids opportunities to accomplish more than they ever thought possible!

TIME FOCUS: VARIES, DEPENDING ON THE PROJECT.

NUMBER OF STUDENTS: UNLIMITED.

Around the Town

Focus of the Fun: Kids will organize a way to send a flying disc from church to church, then discuss how God's love is passed around to others.

Supplies: Flying discs, a local phone book, a local map, and Bibles.

Say: **The object of this project is to send a flying disc from church to church, eventually ending up back at our church. To do this, we will need to enlist other churches who will organize their people into a chain to toss the disc along the distance from one church to another.**

Young-Teenager Tip: Here's a new term (compliments of *Fun Bible-Learning Projects for Young Teenagers*) to add to your youth ministry dictionary: "High Goof Factor (HGF)," n., 1. willingness to contribute silliness and creativity to a group. 2. ability to take an ordinary event and make it fun! Your junior high kids have it. Use it!

Have kids select a date to hold the disc-tossing, as well as an alternate date. Then have junior highers look at the phone book and a map to select five or six churches they'd like to involve in this project. (If kids are willing to be adventurous, have them contact even more churches.) Assign teams to approach each church, explain the activity, and determine a date. Have kids explain that they want to toss a flying disc from one church to the next as a symbol of the unity of the churches in the community and as a reminder to spread God's Word around the community.

Have kids help coordinate where people will stand to toss the flying disc from church to church. The more church members involved at each church, the easier this activity is to accomplish. Between any two churches, it's likely people will have to toss the disc more than once, so tell them it's OK to move from their original positions.

At each church, have the pastor or another person sign the disc and list a favorite Scripture reference about sharing God's Word. Have a support team drive along the route with additional flying discs in case a disc gets lost, run over, or eaten by a dog!

Once the disc has made it back to your church, have kids discuss the following questions: **What was it like to send this disc around such a large area? How is the "bigness" of this project like the bigness of the world we live in? In what ways is this disc-tossing event like the way people hear about God?**

Have kids close the session by reading Matthew 28:16-20 and praying for each other to boldly spread God's Word to the people of their community.

Have each of the participating churches display the flying disc for a week as a reminder to reach out to the community.

Scriptures for Deeper Study: John 15:12; Acts 4:12.

Big Words

Focus of the Fun: Junior highers and middle schoolers will write a giant faith message on an open field and have it photographed from above.

Supplies: Camera, Bibles.

For this project, you'll need a site where kids can spread out on the ground and form letters with their bodies. Choose a field near a tall, climbable tree or tall building so someone can photograph the kids spelling their message.

When you announce this project, tell kids all to wear the same color clothes (white, yellow, or red work well) and to bring lots of friends. You'll also need a camera that allows you to take multiple exposures.

When kids arrive, have them read Colossians 1:3-6 and 1 Corinthians 1:4-9. Ask: **Why does Paul express his thanks and encouragement to the Colossian and Corinthian Christians? What role does encouragement play in the church? What are the best words of encouragement you've received?**

Have kids brainstorm short phrases of encouraging words they'd like to give to the rest of the church. Then take kids to the field where they'll spell out one of the phrases. Explain that kids will be spelling the words by forming letters with their bodies. Have kids then brainstorm ways to form the letters in their phrase. Have a volunteer or two climb the tree or look out the building window and signal kids when they've figured out a good way to do each letter.

Then have kids determine how many words they can spell at a time and mark the ground so they can move to the appropriate places (and spell more words) to form the rest of the phrase. Have the photographer let kids know when he or she has taken a picture (and it's time for them to move again). If the kids have planned appropriately, the entire phrase will be spelled out on the multiple-exposure picture that kids can have enlarged and placed in the church foyer. Kids may want to spell out more than one phrase, or even "draw" a picture in the same way.

Scriptures for Deeper Study: Psalm 31:24; Acts 20:28.

Billboard Campaign

Focus of the Fun: Kids will make billboards that communicate the gospel to a broad audience.

Supplies: A sheet of newsprint, tape, markers, four sheets of poster board, eight 6-foot long wooden stakes, a heavy-duty stapler and staples, a sledgehammer (for hammering in the wooden stakes), and four Bibles.

Have kids form four groups. Have each group read Acts 13:44-49 then discuss the following question: **What do you imagine that Paul and Barnabas experienced as they shared the gospel with such a large group of people?** Have each group share their answers with the larger group. Ask: **If you were to communicate one truth about Jesus Christ to a broad audience, what would you share?**

Say: **Today we are going to create billboards to share the good news of Jesus Christ with our community.** Have kids brainstorm a four-part message that they can communicate to others. For example, they could create a four-part message like the following:

1. "Had a rough day?"
2. "Then may we say..."
3. "You can't go astray..."
4. "With Jesus the Way!"

Write the kids' ideas on a sheet of newsprint taped to a wall.

When the group has agreed on one four-part message they want to share, have them create each part on one sheet of poster board. Assign one part to each group. Tell kids to write their messages boldly and clearly so people will be able to read them from their cars. Make the billboards similar in appearance so people will understand that they belong together. For example, use bright yellow poster board and black marker to create each billboard.

When the kids have finished writing the messages, have them place one stake on each side of the back of the poster board with the pointed side of the stakes extending from the bottom of the poster board. Use the stapler to staple the poster board to the stakes through the front of the sign.

Then have kids decide where they want to place their billboards. For example, they may want to place them 100 yards apart on a well-traveled highway. To do this, get permission from your city, county, or state government department in charge of roads, streets, or highways (depending upon who oversees that highway). Or the group could find a street where they know four families who live on the same side of the road. Have the group ask these families for permission to place the billboards in their front yards so the billboards are visible from the street. Assure the people who agree to help you that the group will remove the billboards after one month. Put the removal date on your calendar and have kids sign up to be on the removal committee.

When the group has decided where to put their billboards, transport the group and the billboards to the four locations. Have the students place their billboards in the order they should appear.

During the month, occasionally ask your group members if they have heard any remarks about the billboards. Check on the billboards periodically to make sure they are still standing.

Scriptures for Deeper Study: Matthew 5:1-12; Acts 3:11-16.

Car Parts

Focus of the Fun: Kids will create a sculpture of a human using old car parts, to illustrate the different parts that make up the body of Christ.

Supplies: Wood, nails, hammers, rope, car parts, and Bibles.

Before the project, have kids go with you to an auto junkyard or dump to collect car parts. Check with the proprietor of the auto junkyard ahead of time to see if he or she will donate the car parts to your group.

When kids return to the church, determine where you'll create your sculpture. You'll need a large area. Have kids use the parts they've collected to create a sculpture of a person. Help kids who like to work with wood use 2×4s and nails to build a large, human-shaped frame. The bigger the frame, the better. You'll want to make sure the structure is safe by adding any support beams that might be necessary.

When the frame is complete, have kids figure out the best placement for the car parts and attach them to the frame using the rope. As kids work, have them discuss the following questions: **Which of the car parts here do you most feel like? Explain. How is this collection of car parts like the members of our church? What gives these car parts value and purpose? What gives the church purpose?**

Have someone read aloud 1 Corinthians 12:12-31 while kids continue working. Then ask: **How can we work together as one body to proclaim the good news and support one another in love? How is this sculpture like a picture of the church?**

After kids complete the sculpture, have them create a sign explaining the significance of the design or quoting a section of 1 Corinthians 12.

Scriptures for Deeper Study: Romans 12:3-8.

Concert Promotion

Focus of the Fun: Kids will promote a Christian concert.

Supplies: One Bible per student, newsprint, masking tape, and markers.

Choose a target date for your concert and begin preparations six months before that date. If possible, choose a holiday or a Saturday so your kids will be available all day to prepare for the concert.

Gather your kids together for a planning meeting. Have kids read Ephesians 5:18-20 in unison. Ask: **What are some ways that music has been meaningful in your relationship with Christ? How did music make that impact on you? What is one specific song that is meaningful to you?**

Say: **To fulfill Ephesians 5:18-20, we are going to promote a concert for one of our favorite Christian artists.** Have kids brainstorm artists they would like to see in concert. Write their ideas on a sheet of newsprint taped to the wall. Then have the group choose three artists from the list. Choose artists who are popular among the youth in your area, who haven't performed in the area for a year, and whose costs you can realistically cover.

Form the following committees to fulfill all of the duties to make the concert work (have one adult leader responsible for overseeing each team).

Artist-Relations Committee:

● Call the agents of the three artists you have chosen to determine availability and financial requirements for having these artists perform. Choose one of the three artists and make the necessary arrangements with the agent, such as signing a contract. You may need to readjust your concert date to accommodate the artist. You can obtain artists' agents names, phone numbers, and addresses in the "Artists•Artist Services•Ministry Organizations" section of the *Christian Music Networking Guide* put out annually by the Gospel Music Association. (The address for the Gospel Music Association is: 7 Music Circle North, Nashville, TN 37203.)

● Determine arrival times and hotel arrangements for the artist. Make sure the hotel is reserved and prepaid for the artist.

● Arrange for meals for all people associated with the artist's arrival.

● Be available the day of the concert to run errands for the artist.

Accounting Committee:

● Recruit financial back up for the concert. Call Christian organizations and bookstores to sponsor the concert in exchange for advertising. You may also have wealthy church members who would be willing to help financially.

● Determine the price of tickets. Concert promoter Michael Scanland says, "When pricing your tickets be sure that your price is high enough that if you sell the concert out, that you have enough revenue to cover all expense plus make 20 to 30 percent profit of the gross receipts."

● Count up all receipts from ticket outlet sales, door sales, and any concession sales.

● Pay all bills involved with the concert, such as the printing company, the artist, and any rentals.

Properties Committee:

● Find and confirm a concert hall in writing. Some artists may perform at your church if your sanctuary can hold a big crowd.

● Recruit a crew of around 45 people to help unload and load artist equipment, usher, sell T-shirts, and run electrical equipment such as spotlights.

● Help with loading on and off stage before and after the concert.

Ticket Sales Committee:
● Have tickets designed and printed. Concert promoter Michael Scanland suggests recruiting a local business to pick up the cost of printing in exchange for having their logo somewhere on each ticket.

● Arrange with 12 to 15 Christian bookstores to sell concert tickets. Distribute promotional materials and tickets to these outlets 12 weeks before the concert.

● Check ticket outlets every three days to determine the number of tickets sold, and redistribute tickets among ticket outlets so that no one runs out. Scanland emphasizes that no one ticket outlet should ever say that the concert is sold out just because they have no tickets. Tell ticket outlets to suggest other outlets until tickets can be redistributed.

● Pick up remaining tickets on the day before the concert.

● Recruit people to sell and take tickets at the concert. Set up a table as a ticket booth, have tickets available, and get a cash box full of enough coins and small bills to make change.

Publicity Committee:
● Work with the artist-relations team to set a definite concert date. Check with other churches, Christian organizations, and Christian radio stations for conflicting events.

● As soon as the artist has been chosen and the date set, begin a word-of-mouth campaign by calling churches and other Christian organizations within a 150-mile radius. Tell them to put the date on their calendars.

● Design and print a poster with all the details. Send a copy to each of the churches you called and to local Christian retailers.

● Begin a mailing campaign 14 weeks before the concert. Design a flier with all of the pertinent information and mail the flier to all churches within a 150-mile radius. Call your post office to determine the requirements for bulk-rate mailing. Concert promoter Mike Scanland suggests calling mailing services, also found in the "Artists•Artist Services•Ministry Organizations" section of the *Christian Music Networking Guide*, which can provide mailing labels for all the churches in your area.

● Six weeks before the concert, send announcements to activity calendars, church bulletins, newspapers, schools, youth programs, and any other free publicity outlets available to you.

● Contact Christian radio stations for advertising rates and possible discounts. Contact all radio stations about advertising through public service announcements. Begin radio advertisements four weeks before the concert.

● Three weeks before the concert, send press releases to religion and entertainment editors of your local newspapers.

● Arrange for the artist to give an interview to one or more of the Christian radio stations on the day of the concert.

Michael Scanland's article "Everything You Ever Wanted to Know about Concert Promotion" in the 1994 *Christian Music Networking Guide* is an excellent source for more information. Consider obtaining a copy of this publication for extra details about concert promotion.

On the day of the concert, gather your concert promotion team together to reread Ephesians 5:18-20. Have the group pray for the concert to fulfill that passage.

After the concert, write thank you notes to all committee members.

> **Young-Teenager Tip:**
> Give your junior highers and middle schoolers plenty of space to roam in your youth program. Include lots of outdoor activities as well as regular indoor meetings. Young teenagers are often sensitive about people getting too close to their "personal space" and need to have time when they don't feel crowded.

Encourage committees to get together to write thank you notes to any people and businesses who helped or donated funds.

Scriptures for Deeper Study: 1 Chronicles 13:6-8; Psalm 150; Colossians 3:16.

Day of 1,000 Balloons

Focus of the Fun: Kids will give away 1,000 balloons to illustrate the impact of sharing the gospel one by one.

Supplies: 1,000 balloons, a helium tank with enough helium to fill 1,000 balloons (look under the heading "Balloons" in the Yellow Pages to find a store that rents helium tanks), 1,000 yards of string, Bibles.

Call shopping center management for permission to set up at a designated area to inflate and give away the balloons.

Arrange to have kids meet at the shopping center. Say: **We are going to see if we can give away 1,000 balloons to kids today.**

Form trios. Have one trio form an assembly line process in which one person fills the balloon, another knots the end, and the third ties one yard of string to the balloon knot. Have the other trios give the balloons away by wandering through the shopping center with bunches of balloons in their hands. Rotate the trios so that each trio has a turn filling and tying the balloons and giving balloons away. Remind trios to give only one balloon to each person.

When the group has given away all of the balloons, ask: **What did it feel like to give away these balloons to the children? How did the children respond? What fun stories do you have from giving away balloons today? What did it feel like to see children wandering around the shopping center with balloons that you had given them? What was it like to see more and more children throughout the day carrying balloons?**

Have trios read John 1:35-51. Have each trio think of one way that the balloon activity was like Jesus' calling the disciples in this passage. Have each trio share their answer with the larger group. Ask: **How can we apply what we learned today, through giving balloons away one by one, to sharing Jesus Christ with those around us?**

Scriptures for Deeper Study: Matthew 4:18-25.

Fill 'er Up

Focus of the Fun: Kids will learn about what "crowds" them in life as they fill a room with clothes, then spend time in the crowded room.

Supplies: Masking tape and Bibles. Kids will collect clothes.

Begin this event by having kids collect clothing, in good condition, from church members and neighbors. For this project to work best, kids will need to collect these items over a number of weeks. Explain that the object is to collect enough clothing items to fill a room (choose a small room in your church to store the items).

Use masking tape to mark off a space in the room where no clothes will be placed. This is where kids will meet once the room is mostly filled.

When the rest of the room is filled, invite kids to a meeting in the space that's left. Lead a regular meeting if possible. Then have kids discuss the following questions: **What is it like to meet in such a small space? Who might feel this way in real life? What kinds of things "crowd" people?**

Read James 1:25 and 2 Corinthians 3:17. Then ask: **What is the freedom talked about in these passages? How can we share that freedom with others? How is the way we're helping others an example of sharing God's freedom?**

Have kids help you package and deliver the clothing to a local welfare agency.

Scriptures for Deeper Study: John 8:32; Psalms 119:32; 146:7.

5,000 Feedings

Focus of the Fun: Kids will develop a program to feed 5,000 people and discuss Jesus' miracle of feeding the 5,000.

Supplies: Newsprint, markers, masking tape, and Bibles.

Say: **We are going to create a program to feed 5,000 people in a unique way.** Tape a sheet of newsprint to a wall and write down kids' ideas as they brainstorm ways to feed 5,000 people. Some possible ideas include:

● Collect money to sponsor 5,000 children for a year through an agency such as Compassion International or World Vision. Recruit people at church to pledge to sponsor one child for the year. Or do some of your favorite fund-raising projects to raise the money. Or do both!

● Coordinate a free-lunch program for 5,000 people over the course of a year. Find a population of needy people that you can serve, such as people at a homeless shelter or at a children's school in a poor area of your community. Create a tentative weekly menu, price the necessary food and drink items, and determine your weekly financial need to do this project. Call local businesses to generate financial support for this project. Create a calendar for people to participate weekly in the project for purchasing food, making sandwiches, and filling lunch bags.

● Purchase 5,000 bite-size candy bars and see how long it takes to give them away (only one per person) to people in your community.

● Bake 20,000 cookies, wrap by fours in cellophane, tie the cellophane with gift ribbon, and deliver the cookies to 5,000 people (for example, church members, hospital patients, shut-ins, or college students).

When you have completed the project the group chooses, have a wrap-up discussion. Ask: **When we started this project, what did you think about feeding 5,000? What was it really like for you to feed 5,000?**

Have kids read Mark 6:32-44 silently to themselves. Ask: **Having fed 5,000** yourselves, what do you think it was like for the disciples to see Jesus feeding 5,000? What have you learned about this miracle that Jesus performed? How do you compare our ability to feed 5,000 with Jesus' ability to feed 5,000? What can we learn from this project and from the Bible passage about how God takes care of our needs?

Scriptures for Deeper Study: Matthew 14:13-21; Luke 9:10-17; John 6:5-14.

God's House T-Shirts

Focus of the Fun: Kids will examine the unity among churches as they design a T-shirt with logos from area churches.

Supplies: T-shirts, phone books, a photocopier with zoom capabilities, paper, and Bibles.

Say: **We're going to design a T-shirt that includes the logos of all the churches in our community, as a sign of our unity in God's work.**

Go through the local phone book and have kids volunteer to contact churches in the community, so that each church is contacted about the possibility of using their church logo on a T-shirt. Have kids explain that they're going to design the shirts and wear them to show their support for the whole church and its mission.

Kids will need to collect a black and white copy of each church's logo after they get permission to use the logo. Then have kids work together to re-size the logos (using a photocopier with zoom capabilities) and place them all on one or two sheets of paper that will become the T-shirt design. Kids may also want to add a slogan such as "We're all in the family of God" or "We're in this together."

Take the design to a local silk-screening business (along with the plain T-shirts) and have the store print the design on the T-shirts. There will be a charge for the silk-screening, but the more shirts done, the cheaper it will be. Have kids ask (but not pressure) the other churches if they want to order shirts. Don't use this as a money-making venture. Everyone who buys a shirt should pay cost only.

When the shirts are complete, spend part of a meeting debriefing the experience. Ask: **What was it like to involve other churches in this project? How were you received by the other churches? How is this a good or bad example of what it means to be in the church of God together?**

After reading John 17:20-23, have kids close in prayer. Ask kids to pray for the leaders and members of each church. Then tell kids to pray for the churches each time they wear the T-shirts.

Scriptures for Deeper Study: Psalm 133; Romans 15:5; Ephesians 4:3, 13; Colossians 3:14.

Grand Coverup

Focus of the Fun: Kids will disguise a local landmark and discuss the effects of trying to cover up sin.

Supplies: One sheet of newsprint, masking tape, a marker, an instant-print camera and film, paper, pencils, and Bibles.

Think of a well-known building, landmark, or statue in your community that the group could disguise. Get permission from the building owners or from city hall to temporarily disguise the building, landmark, or statue.

Say: **We are going to see if we can disguise** (name of building, landmark, or statue) **in such a way that no one will recognize it. Let's think of ways we could temporarily disguise this structure.** Have the group brainstorm ways to disguise the building, landmark, or statue, and write their ideas on a sheet of newsprint taped to the wall. Emphasize that this project is temporary and that the group won't permanently deface the structure. Some possible ideas for disguising a structure:

● dress a well-known statue in trendy clothing, place sunglasses on its face, and put a wig on top;

● drape sheets over recognizable parts of a building and use clay to change the letters on a sign into other letters spelling another word; or

● use poster board cut in shapes of eyes, nose, mouth, and ears, and use duct tape to attach them to a well-known rock.

When the group has determined a way to disguise the structure, gather the necessary supplies and put the plan into action. Take four pictures of the finished product. Have kids form four groups. Give each group paper and pencils and send each group to one of four places in the community (for example, outside a supermarket, in a shopping center, outside a library, or on a street corner) and ask people whether they can identify the structure. Have kids record their answers on their papers.

When the groups return, have them share the results of their survey, sharing how many people correctly identified the structure and what some of the incorrect answers were.

Have the group read Proverbs 28:13 aloud in unison. Ask: **How is this passage like our grand coverup activity? Think of one thing you did in your past that you knew was wrong and tried to cover up. How did you feel when someone discovered the coverup? How did you feel when you got away with the coverup? What does this passage say to you about covering up our wrongdoing? How will you change the way you deal with your mistakes based on what we learned through our project?**

Scriptures for Deeper Study: Psalms 38; 51.

Young-Teenager Tip: Running into snags while planning a junior high event? Then laugh! According to GROUP Magazine, laughter:

● gives a soothing massage to almost all your body's organs,

● strengthens your immune system,

● makes stress manageable,

● improves your circulation and breathing,

● acts as a natural painkiller,

● makes you more alert,

● speeds up your metabolism and helps you digest your food, and

● stimulates creative, right-brain thinking. ("Hands on Help: Personal Life," GROUP Magazine)

In the Lions' Den

Focus of the Fun: Kids will decorate the inside of the church to look like a lions' den, then lead a study on Daniel for the whole congregation.

Supplies: Audiocassette player and blank tape, butcher paper, tape, markers, paint and paintbrushes, a camera (optional) and Bibles.

Have kids read aloud Daniel 6 (the story of Daniel in the lions' den). Ask: **What are the main themes in this story? How has God answered one of your prayers? How does God protect us today?**

Say: **To help our church know what Daniel might have felt like, we're going to decorate the sanctuary to look like a lions' den.** If your sanctuary is too large to decorate, choose another room and plan on having kids lead a meeting with the whole congregation in that room.

Form teams to work on the different aspects of the decoration. Team 1 will determine how to create life-size (or larger) lions. Team 2 will determine how to make the sanctuary walls look like a den. How to use sound to make the den seem real will be the task of Team 3. Team 4 will figure out how to create the illusion that crowds of people are peering down into the den.

Give kids the supplies and have them begin work on the transformation of your sanctuary. Here are a few ideas to get kids started.

● Cut out life-size lions from the butcher paper and tape them all around the room on the walls.

● Cover the entire wall with butcher paper painted to look like a stone wall.

● Draw faces on butcher paper and tape them around the room on the top of the "stone wall."

● Record a multitude of lions' roars for the background sounds.

When the room is complete, have kids lead a discussion with the whole congregation on the story of Daniel in the lions' den. Have kids come up with questions to ask people about the story and about how it applies to their own lives. Be sure to take lots of photos of the finished room.

If your kids enjoyed this activity, consider doing a similar one later in the year. For example, kids could decorate the room to look like the belly of a huge fish and plan a discussion on what it's like to run from God. Or kids could decorate the room to look like the Red Sea when it was parted for the Israelites to cross over and plan a discussion on how God protects us.

Scriptures for Deeper Study: Jonah; Exodus 14.

Land of the Giants

Focus of the Fun: Kids will learn about childlikeness as they create larger-than-life props.

Supplies: Wood pieces, nails, hammers, cardboard, tape, paint and paintbrushes, markers, camera (optional), and Bibles.

Form groups of no more than six and have each group choose one item that they'd like to build in giant size (as if creating props for a "land of the giants" film). For example, kids might create a huge chair, a giant toothbrush, a big telephone, a larger-than-life table, or a towering television. Show kids the supplies and have each group explain how it would create the giant prop. Then help kids begin work on their giant props (the bigger they are, the better).

Note: This activity works best if you have a few "crafty" adults on hand to help kids with the design and construction of the items.

As kids work on the items, have them discuss when they've felt "small" in life. Go around and help kids as they build and decorate their giant props.

When the props are done, have kids stand in front of them for a photo. Then have kids sit near the items. Ask: **How is looking at these items like the way children might feel as they look around their "grown-up" world? How does it feel to be small?**

Have volunteers read aloud Matthew 19:14-15. Ask: **Why does Jesus want the children to come to him? What aspects of childlikeness should we have in our lives? What are ways we can include children in our lives? How can our examples of faith help children to not fear the "big world" of the grownups?**

Save your big props for possible future use in a skit or in a meeting for the adults in your church on the theme of "becoming like a child" or "seeing things through a child's eyes."

Scriptures for Deeper Study: Psalm 127:3; Proverbs 17:6; Isaiah 54:13.

Life-Size Storybook

Focus of the Fun: Kids will create a living Bible storybook to share with others.

Supplies: Bibles, two refrigerator boxes, a roll of butcher paper or a pad of newsprint, masking tape, pencils, tempera paints, paintbrushes, yarn, and scissors.

Say: **We are going to create a life-size living Bible storybook. We as a group need to decide which story to tell.** Have the group think of their favorite Bible stories and agree on one to create in life-size form. For example, the group could tell a story about a favorite Bible character or tell one of Jesus' parables. Have the group decide what audience to target. For example, you could tell the story to a children's Sunday school class or support your pastor's sermon based on the same passage and target the story for an adult congregation.

When the group has chosen a story and audience, form three committees.

Story Committee: Rewrites the story in familiar, everyday language with a narrator describing the action. This committee also determines the number of scenes the Painting Committee will need to create.

Painting Committee: Cuts refrigerator boxes into "pages" that measure 6×3 feet. Next they cover each piece of cardboard by taping butcher paper or newsprint to it. They paint a title page and each scene on a separate piece of covered cardboard. (Kids may want to sketch out their scenes in pencil first.)

Blocking Committee: Determines where people will stand while the story is told.

Have the group collectively determine the message they would like to communicate. For example, if the group chooses to tell the parable of the Good Samaritan as told in Luke 10:30-35, the Story Committee would rewrite the story to suit the intended audience and could determine that there are two scenes for the Paint Committee to create. The Paint Committee could create a title page that says "The Good Samaritan" or "Love Your Neighbor." The Paint Committee could also create a road scene and an inn scene. The Blocking Committee would look at the script written by the Story Committee and determine where the narrator would stand, where the attacked man would lie in the scene, where the priest and Levite would walk, and other actions described in the story. At the end of the story, the Story Committee could summarize the lesson, such as "Love your neighbor as you love yourself."

When all of the scenes have been created and the paint has dried, have kids use scissors to bore two holes, 2 inches in from the left side of each scene, with one hole 2 feet from the top and the other 2 feet from the bottom. Then have the kids stack the scenes on top of each other in order. Have some students cut two 1-foot pieces of yarn and put one through the top set of holes and the other through the bottom set of holes. Tie each piece of yarn into a double knot to bind the book.

When the group has finished the book, have them perform their life-size storybook for their intended audience. Ask students to share with each other what they learned about God while creating this story and communicating a biblical message to others.

Scriptures for Deeper Study: Luke 8:9-10.

Prayer for the World

Focus of the Fun: Group members will draw a giant map of the world, then lead congregation members in praying for people in other countries.

Supplies: Sheets of poster board, tape, pencils, markers, a map of the world, and Bibles.

Tell kids they're going to create a floor-size map of the world in one of the church rooms. Choose a room with a solid-surface floor and enough space to house your entire congregation.

Have kids cover the floor with sheets of poster board by taping pieces together, edge to edge. Then have group members refer to a large map of the world and re-create that map on the floor. Kids should use pencil at first as they figure out how big to make each continent.

One way to simplify the drawing process is to divide the floor into a grid by drawing parallel lines both vertically and horizontally on the paper. Then, after drawing the same lines on the reference map and taping it to the wall, assign one or more sections for each person to copy on the floor map. Kids can refer to the map on a wall in the room to know what to draw. When the map has been drawn, have kids use markers to outline the countries and write the names of the countries in the appropriate places.

When the map is done, have kids lead the whole congregation in walking around the world and praying for the people in each country they "visit." Someone might also read aloud James 5:13-18 as a part of the prayer service.

When the project is done, have each person choose a continent to sit on for a brief discussion of the activity. Have kids discuss the following questions with people sitting on their continent: **How is the effort and care we took in making this map like the effort and care missionaries take in reaching the people around the world? What are ways we can support Christians around the world?**

Have each person collect one or more sections of the map and plan on praying for the people in that country during the coming weeks. For fun, see if kids still have their pieces of the map in a few months and have a map puzzle party where kids try to put it back together again.

Scriptures for Deeper Study: Matthew 28:19; 1 Thessalonians 5:16-17; John 17:13-24.

Radio Show

Focus of the Fun: Kids will record a "radio show" featuring music, talk shows, skits, and other elements, then share the recorded show with school friends.

Supplies: Audiocassette recorders, blank audiocassette tapes, and Bibles.

Form groups of no more than four and have each group choose one of the following elements of a radio show that they'd like to work on: talk show, music, radio drama, or commercial. Be sure all aspects of the show are selected (more than one group can work on the same element).

Say: **We're going to create a radio show about what it means to be a Christian. We'll distribute our show to non-Christian friends. The object of each group is to create a portion of a radio show that would appeal to kids your age using the format you chose.**

For example, the talk show group might have a group member be a talk show host for a discussion on the difficulty of being a Christian in non-Christian world. The music group might choose a group member to act as DJ and introduce a series of songs about a particular faith theme. The commercial group might create a commercial for the youth group, the church, or simply advertise the benefits of being a Christian. And the radio drama group could write a skit illustrating the false impressions of Christianity that many non-Christians have.

Give kids plenty of time to work on their portions of the radio show. Suggest that kids also include Scripture where appropriate in the show. For example, the talk show might include a discussion of a particular Scripture passage and what it means to kids.

Help kids arrange the elements in a logical order and choose someone to act as the DJ for the whole project. This person will need to introduce the idea, then tie the elements together as a real radio DJ might.

When kids are ready, record the various sections of the show. It's OK to do multiple "takes" if necessary. Kids will want the best possible finished product to give their friends.

When the tape is complete, listen to it with your group. Then make copies of the tape for kids to share with friends.

Scriptures for Deeper Study: 2 Timothy 4:2; 1 Corinthians 1:17.

Simultaneous Chorus of Praise

Focus of the Fun: Group members will coordinate the singing of a familiar praise song in a variety of churches in the community at the same time.

Supplies: Songbooks (such as *Group's Praise & Worship Songbook* from Group Publishing), audiocassette recorders, blank audiocassette tapes, a phone book or list of area churches, and Bibles.

Have volunteers define the word "praise." Then have kids read Psalms 34 and 150. Form pairs and ask: **Why do we praise God? What role should praise play in our church? in our private faith lives? How do we praise God?**

Say: **One of the most common ways to praise God is through music, so we're going to lead our community in praising God in song.**

Have kids choose a familiar praise song (such as "Awesome God") that most church members in the community would know. Then assign each pair to call one or more churches from the phone book or from a list of area churches. These pairs will be responsible for explaining to the churches the "Simultaneous Chorus of Praise" activity. Explain that the community-wide chorus of praise is simply a time when all church members around the city will sing the same praise song at the same time.

Choose a day and time when you want to lead this activity. A weekday evening works, but a Sunday morning may be the best choice. Then have kids call their assigned churches and explain the event purpose (to promote unity in the church and to praise God together). If possible, get a local Christian radio station to play your praise song at precisely the agreed-upon time.

Ask church leaders to explain to their congregations what's going on just before they sing the praise song together. Also, have kids provide tape recorders to each church (or make sure they have one available) to record the chorus of praise.

Scriptures for Deeper Study: Psalms 100:4; 107:8; Luke 2:13-14.

Wall Building

Focus of the Fun: Kids will surround an area with an 8-foot wall and discuss breaking down walls between people.

Supplies: Cardboard boxes, masking tape, duct tape, four stepladders, and Bibles.

Select an area to enclose with a cardboard-box wall (for example, the youth office, someone's house, or a student's yard). Obtain permission from whoever owns the building to construct this wall temporarily. Measure the perimeter of the area you will enclose. Collect enough boxes to use as bricks to completely surround the area with an 8-foot wall. For example, if the building is 100×50 feet, you will need at least 1,200 2×1-foot boxes to construct an 8-foot wall.

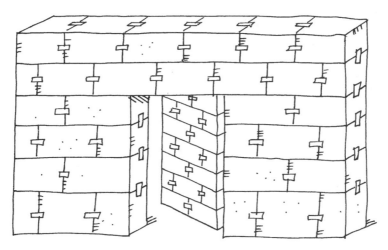

Have kids collaborate to stack the boxes like bricks and tape them together with the masking tape. Have your students continue this until they have surrounded the building with a wall of boxes, leaving an opening for a gate. Construct the gate by stacking some boxes into a door, creating a hinge with a strip of duct tape running down one side of the door. Secure the hinge by taping 1-foot strips of duct tape horizontally over the hinge. Construct sentry posts around the wall by leaving a space in the top of the wall for someone to look through. Then place one of the stepladders inside the wall at that point for the sentry to stand on.

When the group has completed the wall, ask: **What purpose do walls serve? How does it feel to be inside our wall? How does it feel to be outside? What are some ways we build walls between us and other people? Why do we do this? What are some reasons for breaking down walls between us and others? What are some ways we can accomplish this?**

Have the group read John 17:20-23 aloud in unison. Ask: **Based on this passage, what do you think Jesus would say about us building or breaking down walls between us and others? What is one way you can break down a wall with someone this week?**

Have the group gather in a circle. One by one have each student take one box from the wall and give it to another student. Have the giver share how he or she has seen the receiver break down a wall between people. Make sure each student gives away one box and receives one box.

Scriptures for Deeper Study: Joshua 6:1-27; John 10:14-16; 1 Corinthians 3:3-9.

Youth Group Pen Pals

Focus of the Fun: Corresponding with other youth groups.

Supplies: Bibles, paper, pencils, first-class postage stamps, newsprint, tape, markers in assorted colors, a camera, film, and manila envelopes.

Use this project to help your kids make contact with other youth groups in the country.

Ask: **When you write a letter to someone, what do you communicate to that person? When you receive a letter from someone, what do you like to hear from that person? How does exchanging letters with someone affect your relationship?**

Have kids form pairs. Give each pair a Bible, a sheet of paper, and a pencil. Have pairs read 1 John 1:1-4 and list the various elements of this part of John's letter. Tape a sheet of newsprint to the wall. Have pairs share with the group what they wrote on their lists and write their responses on the newsprint.

Say: **We are going to initiate a youth group pen pal system. We will recruit 12 other youth groups in 12 different states to exchange letters every month with one other youth group on the list.**

Have kids share names of their friends who are in other states who also attend youth groups. You can also share your connections with youth ministers and friends in other states. When the group has constructed a list of 13 youth groups (including your own), from 13 different states, have the group create one letter to copy and send to the other 12 churches. In the letter, ask the other youth groups if they want to be involved in the youth group pen pal system. Include a church-addressed postcard on which they can check a "yes" or "no" box for being involved. Include the following details in your letter.

● This project is a youth group-to-youth group pen pal system (not individuals writing to each other but youth groups exchanging one giant letter with the other groups).

● Each group will write to one other group each month.

● Each month the youth groups will write to a different youth group.

● Letters can include reports on events happening in the youth group, news on current events in the state, school pictures, pictures from youth events, funny stories about group activities, questions about how to handle problems, suggestions on how to handle problems, ideas for unique youth group activities that were successful, or any other elements the group wishes to include.

● The pen pal groups may initiate a theme month, such as "Elvis Month," and youth groups have to tell that month's youth group pen pal how they celebrated the theme. For example, a youth group may write that they had an Elvis look-alike contest, an Elvis song lip-sync contest, a peanut butter and banana sandwich-eating contest, or any other unique way they celebrated the theme. Include pictures of the events. To initiate such a theme month, a youth group sends postcards to all other youth groups in the pen pal system to proclaim the theme and explain the rules.

When you receive the postcards back from youth groups, make a list of the

Youth Group Pen Pals

Names of 13 churches written in the same order on both axes

	Church of Denver	Church of New York	Church of Boston	Church of Lincoln	Church of San Francisco	Church of Dallas	Church of Boise	Church of Seattle	Church of Charleston	Church of Charlotte	Church of Detroit	Church of Chicago	Church of Cheyenne
Church of Denver	■	Jan.	Feb.	Mar.	Apr.	May	Jun.	Jul.	Aug.	Sep.	Oct.	Nov.	Dec.
Church of New York	Dec.	■	Jan.	Feb.	Mar.	Apr.	May	Jun.	Jul.	Aug.	Sep.	Oct.	Nov.
Church of Boston	Nov.	Dec.	■	Jan.	Feb.	Mar.	Apr.	May	Jun.	Jul.	Aug.	Sep.	Oct.
Church of Lincoln	Oct.	Nov.	Dec.	■	Jan.	Feb.	Mar.	Apr.	May	Jun.	Jul.	Aug.	Sep.
Church of San Francisco	Sep.	Oct.	Nov.	Dec.	■	Jan.	Feb.	Mar.	Apr.	May	Jun.	Jul.	Aug.
Church of Dallas	Aug.	Sep.	Oct.	Nov.	Dec.	■	Jan.	Feb.	Mar.	Apr.	May	Jun.	Jul.
Church of Boise	Jul.	Aug.	Sep.	Oct.	Nov.	Dec.	■	Jan.	Feb.	Mar.	Apr.	May	Jun.
Church of Seattle	Jun.	Jul.	Aug.	Sep.	Oct.	Nov.	Dec.	■	Jan.	Feb.	Mar.	Apr.	May
Church of Charleston	May	Jun.	Jul.	Aug.	Sep.	Oct.	Nov.	Dec.	■	Jan.	Feb.	Mar.	Apr.
Church of Charlotte	Apr.	May	Jun.	Jul.	Aug.	Sep.	Oct.	Nov.	Dec.	■	Jan.	Feb.	Mar.
Church of Detroit	Mar.	Apr.	May	Jun.	Jul.	Aug.	Sep.	Oct.	Nov.	Dec.	■	Jan.	Feb.
Church of Chicago	Feb.	Mar.	Apr.	May	Jun.	Jul.	Aug.	Sep.	Oct.	Nov.	Dec.	■	Jan.
Church of Cheyenne	Jan.	Feb.	Mar.	Apr.	May	Jun.	Jul.	Aug.	Sep.	Oct.	Nov.	Dec.	■

churches that will participate. If some youth groups decline, have another brainstorming meeting to find other groups that will participate.

When the group has found 12 other youth groups to participate in this pen pal system, create a diagram that explains how groups will switch pen pals throughout the year.

Have kids create 13 pen pal packets. Have kids enclose the following items in each packet: a youth group pen pal diagram, a letter reiterating the guidelines for the pen pal system and telling youth groups to mail their letters in the third week of the month, and a list of the youth group contact people and addresses for each church. Have your group enclose these items in manila envelopes, address each envelope to one youth group in the pen pal system, stamp with the appropriate postage, and mail the packets. Keep one packet for your group.

When you prepare to write a letter to another youth group, have kids brainstorm what they want to communicate to the other youth group. Post the list they created when they read 1 John 1:1-4, and encourage the group to include these elements in their letter. Then have the group write the letter on a sheet of newsprint in colorful markers. Include any pictures you want to share. After the letter is written, seal it in a manila envelope, affix the necessary postage, and mail it!

Young-Teenager Tip: Youth minister Mark Simone suggests four guidelines for maintaining discipline with junior highers: make few rules, set consistent boundaries, explain the rules, and offer choices. (Mark Simone, "No-Fail Discipline," JR. HIGH MINISTRY Magazine)

Scriptures for Deeper Study: 1 Corinthians 16:13-24; Galatians 1:1-5; Philippians 1:1-11; 2 Thessalonians 3:16-18; Philemon; 1 Peter 1:1-2.

6 Holiday Projects

Holidays are special days, so celebrate them in special, unique ways with the projects in this chapter. These projects focus on various holidays such as Valentine's Day, Christmas, and even made-up holidays like Rainbow Day. Not only do these projects cover a variety of holidays, they also focus on Christian truths that kids will remember.

TIME FOCUS: VARIES, DEPENDING ON THE PROJECT.

NUMBER OF STUDENTS: VARIES, DEPENDING ON THE PROJECT.

New Year's Day Flashbacks (January 1)

Focus of the Fun: Kids will relive the previous year's events in reverse order and celebrate the good times they've had together.

Supplies: Newsprint, markers, video camera and film, and Bibles.

Open by reading Philippians 1:3-6. Form pairs and have them discuss the following questions: **Why did Paul include this message in his letter to the Philippian Christians? Why is it important to remember one another in prayer? What is the value of sharing faith experiences with others?**

Say: **New Year's Day is usually considered to be a time of transition, a time to remember past experiences and to move on to new ones. So we're going to remember the events of the past year.**

Have kids begin by brainstorming the significant events of the past year. Write these events on a sheet of newsprint. Then form groups of no more than four to act out the events in reverse order. In other words, the first event to be acted out would be the most recent one. (For example: decorating a Christmas tree, then having Thanksgiving dinner and taking a nap, going trick or treating for Halloween, and so on.) Have someone in each group narrate the activity being acted out and describe what made it a significant event. Record the entire reverse history using a video camera.

When kids have finished their look back, have them create another video. This time, have them act out the events they hope will happen in the coming year. Watch the video with kids after it's completed. Then save the tape until the end of the year and play it again for kids to see how well they predicted the events.

Scriptures for Deeper Study: John 13:34; Psalm 55:14; Proverbs 17:17.

Candy Bouquets
(Valentine's Day, February 14)

Focus of the Fun: Kids will make candy bouquets as a way of showing love to others.

Supplies: One Bible per student; bags of various bite-size candy bars (enough for each student to have six pieces); six bamboo skewers per student (available at grocery stores); a roll of pink cellophane wrap (available at grocery stores); one roll each of red, pink, and white curling gift ribbon; scissors; 9×12-inch sheets of red, pink, and white construction paper; assorted colors of markers; and a hole punch.

Ask: **What does Valentine's Day mean to you? What does the word "love" mean to you?** Have kids read 1 Corinthians 13 to themselves. Ask: **What does this passage say about love? What are ways you have expressed this kind of love during the past week?**

Say: **Today we are going to create candy bouquets for someone we love. You can choose anyone to show love to. It could be a parent, a friend, a teacher, or any other person who is special to you.**

Have each student choose six candy bars. Give each student six bamboo skewers, six 1-foot pieces of pink cellophane, and six 1-foot strips of colored ribbon. Instruct students to push the tip of one skewer halfway through the longest part of one candy bar. Then have them place the candy in the center of one piece of pink cellophane, wrap the cellophane around the candy, and tie the cellophane to the skewer with a piece of gift ribbon. Have them curl the ends of the ribbon by running the edge of the scissors down the length of the ribbon. Tell students to repeat this process with the remaining candy bars, skewers, cellophane, and ribbons. During this process have kids share ways that they have shown 1 Corinthians 13 love to those around them.

Young-Teenager Tip: Did you know that 62 percent of kids ages 8 to 17 think they have the right amount of homework each day? (*100% American* by Daniel Evan Weiss)

When kids have finished creating their candy "flowers," have them create cards out of the construction paper. Remind them to express love toward their chosen person in a way that is consistent with 1 Corinthians 13. When they have finished their cards, have each person punch a hole in the upper left corner. Give each student another 1-foot piece of ribbon to thread through the hole and around all six candy flowers, creating a candy bouquet.

Scriptures for Deeper Study: Proverbs 17:17; Matthew 22:37-40; John 13:34-35.

Equinox Party (about March 21 or September 22)

Focus of the Fun: Group members will host a party for younger children, then discuss light overcoming darkness.

Supplies: Two pieces of newsprint, masking tape, a marker, and Bibles. Other supplies will be determined by the group.

Arrange to have your group members host a party for a younger group in the church on the spring equinox (about March 21) or the autumn equinox (about September 22). Have kids meet a few weeks before the party to plan it.

At your planning meeting, say: **We're going to plan a spring** (autumn) **equinox party for** (the group you will be hosting)**. Because the spring** (autumn) **equinox is a day when it is dark and light the same amount of time during a 24-hour period, our party will be half activities done in the dark and half activities done in the light. So let's brainstorm some ideas.**

Tape both pieces of newsprint to the wall side by side. Across the top of one write "dark" and across the top of the other write "light." Allow kids to brainstorm ideas for both lists. For example, for the dark list, kids could suggest a treasure hunt where they hide items for the group to find in the dark. For a light activity, kids could bring flashlights and see how many flashlights it takes to completely light up the room. Have the group choose three activities from each list and assign people to be in charge of each activity: gathering supplies, introducing the activity, and running the activity.

Have the kids throw the party. After it is over ask: **What were the differences between what we could do in the dark and what we could do in the light? What does it feel like to be in the dark? What does it feel like to be in the light?** Have the group read 1 John 2:8-11 aloud in unison. Ask: **What does this passage say about light and dark? How was this passage true for our Equinox Party? How can you apply this passage to your daily living?**

Scriptures for Deeper Study: Genesis 1:1-5; Psalm 112:4; Romans 13:12; Ephesians 5:8-14.

Tomb Prayer-Closet
(Easter)

Focus of the Fun: Kids will construct a "tomb" and invite church members to visit the tomb and pray during the Easter season.

Supplies: Black paper or plastic, chicken wire, duct tape, a lamp with a dim blue light bulb (or a blue Christmas tree bulb in an electric "candle"), and Bibles.

For this project, kids will need a room that they can use to construct a large "tomb" that will stay up during the Easter season.

Have kids begin by reading Matthew 27:27-66 and discussing the following questions: **What do you think Jesus' disciples were feeling when Jesus was crucified? How would you have felt to see him die? What would it be like to visit the tomb and find it empty? What would your first thoughts be?**

Tell kids they're going to create a large tomb using the supplies you've collected. Say: **This tomb will be a place where people can come during the week to pray in solitude, thanking God for the sacrifice of his Son and asking God to help them focus on the true significance of the Easter season.**

Have kids help you determine a design for the tomb, then build it. For example, kids might shape the chicken wire into a large dome with a small entrance, then cover the dome with thick black plastic, leaving a flap in the front where people can enter the room. When the tomb is complete, have kids place a small blue light in the tomb.

Have kids crowd into the tomb and spend a few minutes in silent prayer, thanking God for the incredible sacrifice of Jesus. Then have kids come out of the tomb. Ask: **What was it like to be in the near-darkness? How is that like the feeling Jesus must've had on the cross? like the feeling the disciples had? How did things change when you exited the tomb? How is that like the way people change when they've met Christ?**

Have kids explain the tomb to your congregation and encourage them to visit it for silent prayer during the Easter season. After Easter, remove the tomb and replace it with a sign that reads "He is risen!"

Scriptures for Deeper Study: Luke 24:30-35; 1 Corinthians 15:12-14; 2 Corinthians 4:14.

Flag Day
(June 14)

Focus of the Fun: Kids will create a youth group flag to illustrate the idea of openly showing allegiance to God.

Supplies: Bibles, two sheets of newsprint, masking tape, marker, pencils, one 3×5-foot piece of fabric (an old sheet cut to size is fine), tacky glue (available at local arts and crafts stores), various colors of felt, scissors, and assorted colors of permanent markers.

Plan to do this project during the week before Flag Day so it will be completed by June 14.

Ask: **What does a flag signify or represent to you? If you had a flag that represented yourself, what would be on it?**

Form pairs. Have pairs read Psalm 20:5 and paraphrase the verse in today's language. Have pairs share their paraphrases with the whole group. Ask: **What does it mean to raise a flag to God?**

Say: **For Flag Day this year, we are going to create our own youth group flag.** Tell kids to brainstorm how they would like their youth group flag to look. For example, the group may want to include a picture of raised hands to signify praising God, or they may want to include a dog as a symbol of faithfulness and obedience. Tape a sheet of newsprint to the wall and list the group's ideas.

When the group has brainstormed a number of ideas, have the group choose one idea to create. Have them collaborate on the design by drawing ideas for the flag on the second sheet of newsprint. When they have decided on a design, have them determine how to create it. They might draw the design on the fabric, and glue or sew felt to it, or draw on it with markers.

On Flag Day, have your group gather in the youth room for a ceremonial raising of their group flag. You can tack the flag to one wall with pushpins. Or you can attach a flag holder to the wall, staple your flag to one end of a dowel (make sure it fits into the flag holder), and put the other end of the dowel into the flag holder. You can find flag holders and dowels at your local hardware store. A third option would be to fly your flag from an already established flag pole. Measure the length between the clips on the rope. Then have someone sew two buttonholes on the left side of the flag at the appropriate distance.

Scriptures for Deeper Study: Exodus 17:15; Song of Solomon 2:4; Isaiah 18:3.

Flag Fest
(Flag Day, June 14)

Focus of the Fun: Kids will celebrate Flag Day by creating flags to represent their own personalities and flying them outside their homes with their American flags.

Supplies: Cloth pieces, markers, and Bibles.

Give each person a 3×4-foot piece of cloth and markers. Have each person create a flag that symbolizes who he or she is.

Encourage kids to include illustrations representing their interests, hobbies, and personalities. For example, someone might draw an airplane to indicate his or her interest in traveling. Or someone might illustrate a scene from a school play to show his or her interest in drama.

When the flags are done, have kids sit in a circle. Ask kids to explain the designs on their flags. Then have kids describe how they feel when they see their nation's flag flying. Say: **Each country's flag represents a unique place, a unique culture, and a unique identity. In a similar way, our flags represent who God has created us to be.**

Have someone read aloud Jeremiah 1:5. Ask: **What is this passage telling us about how God creates people? How does it feel to know that God created you to be unique and valuable? What causes us to feel less than valuable in life? How can we help each other feel good about the one-of-a-kind people we are?**

Have kids fly their personality flags outside their homes on Flag Day.

Scriptures for Deeper Study: Isaiah 49:1-5; 1 Corinthians 12:1-11.

All-in-One Halloween Costume (Halloween, October 31)

Focus of the Fun: Kids will experience unity by creating a single costume that they all will wear simultaneously.

Supplies: One sheet of newsprint, masking tape, markers, a church directory, and Bibles. The rest of the supplies will be determined by the group.

Begin this project two weeks before Halloween to give the group enough time to create the costume.

Say: **For Halloween this year, we are going to create a costume that we can all be a part of.** Have kids brainstorm possible costume ideas that require everyone's participation. For example, they could find some old sheets, sew them together along one side, cut enough holes in a line for everyone to put their heads through facing the same direction, and be a caterpillar. Or they could sew a giant set of overalls so everyone could fit into it and be a multiple-headed person. Or one person could dress up as Bo Peep and the rest could be sheep. Write down all of the group's ideas on newsprint taped to the wall, then have the group choose one costume idea to implement.

Young-Teenager Tip: School activities heat up as kids reach junior high and middle school. Check the schedules for important school events and work around these as much as possible when planning your youth group calendar.

Have kids decide who will be which part of the costume and who will put it together. Plan more meetings for kids to work on the costume. You may want to break the costume into parts and put smaller groups in charge of one part of the costume. For example, if you did the Bo Peep idea, one group would be in charge of getting Bo Peep's costume and another group would create sheep costumes. Make sure everyone gets involved in creating the costume.

On Halloween night, have all the kids get into the costume and go trick or treating at church members' houses, using the church directory to find their addresses. (You may need to arrange transportation for your students if church members live far away from each other.)

When you return to church, have the group get out of the costume and sit in a circle. Have them inspect their candy then dig in! Then discuss the project.

Ask: **What did you experience as we worked together to develop our costume? What did you experience as we trick or treated in one costume? What are other situations in which you have had similar feelings?**

Have kids read Ephesians 4:2-6 aloud in unison. Ask: **What did you see in this passage that applies to tonight's project? What is one thing you can do this week to promote unity in your family, with your friends, or in this group?**

Scriptures for Deeper Study: Psalm 133:1; Acts 2:42-47; 1 Corinthians 12:27; 1 Peter 3:8.

Thanks for You (Thanksgiving)

Focus of the Fun: Junior highers and middle schoolers will find out how congregation members have helped others, then create personalized "thanksgiving messages" to send.

Supplies: Rolls of paper (such as shelf paper), markers, and Bibles.

Form investigative teams of no more than four kids to research ways your congregation members have helped people in need. Assign each team a person you know has been active in helping others. Tell group members to talk with family members about the kinds of things their assigned person does to help out at home, work, or elsewhere. The more specific information kids can get, the better.

Then have kids meet to create personalized banners of thanksgiving to send their helpful people. Have kids create giant thank you notes by using a roll of paper and writing on it a personalized thank you note. For example, the banner might include a line that reads, "Thanks for taking the time to read to your children" or "Thanks for giving so much time to help the people at the homeless shelter." Have teams include as many specific thanksgivings as possible.

On or around Thanksgiving, have kids deliver the large notes by attaching them to the people's front doors or displaying them in the front yards.

When kids have delivered their thankful notes, meet with them to read and discuss Acts 20:35. Ask: **How do your assigned people live out this message? How did we live out this message through this project? What are other ways to live out this message in daily life?**

Scriptures for Deeper Study: 1 Corinthians 12:27-31; Acts 9:36; 1 Timothy 5:3-10.

Thanksgiving-Grams (Thanksgiving)

Focus of the Fun: Kids will deliver a message of thanks to someone who has helped the group.

Supplies: Bibles. The rest of the supplies will be determined by the group.

Arrange for transportation for all of the kids.

Say: **Today we are going to show our gratitude to someone. Who is**

someone who has done something special for our group? Have kids agree on one person. (For example, they might choose a parent, a pastor, an adult leader, or some other person who has helped the youth group in a special way, perhaps by planning an event or transporting the kids to camp.)

Then have the kids think of a special thanksgiving-gram they can send to that person. For example, the group could write a "thank you" song to the tune of "Mary Had a Little Lamb," dress in clown costumes, and deliver the thanksgiving-gram by going to that person's house and performing their song.

When kids have thought of their idea, gather the supplies necessary to implement the idea. Have kids put together costumes, signs to carry that say "Thank You," or anything else that will enhance their delivery. Transport the kids to that person's house and have the kids perform their thanksgiving-gram. (Call first to make sure when the lucky recipient will be home!)

After delivering the thanksgiving-gram, ask: **What was it like for you to show your gratitude to** (name of person)**? Who else are you thankful for? How do you show someone that you are thankful for them?**

Form foursomes and have the foursomes read Psalm 105:1-4, with each person reading one verse. Ask: **What does this passage say about being thankful to God? What is one way you can send a thanksgiving-gram to God for Thanksgiving Day this year?**

Scriptures for Deeper Study: Psalm 116:17; Ephesians 5:19-20; 1 Thessalonians 5:18; Revelation 7:12.

Multimedia Christmas (Advent, December)

Focus of the Fun: Kids will prepare and present a multimedia show on the Christmas story.

Supplies: Bibles, slide projectors, cameras, audiocassette players, and other multimedia equipment.

This project can be completed in just a few weeks. Plan on starting it after Thanksgiving. Explain to kids that they're going to create a multimedia program on the Christmas story to show to the whole church. Spend the first few minutes brainstorming the kinds of things kids might want to include in the multimedia show. Here are a few ideas:

● pictures of how the world views Christmas (lots of presents, Santa, decorated malls),

   ● pictures of young children dressed in shepherd outfits,

   ● staged picture of a nativity scene,

   ● recording of your church choir singing Christmas hymns,

   ● interviews with people about what Christmas means to them, or

   ● skits about the Christmas story.

Together, read Luke 2 and discuss additional elements necessary to communicate the true meaning of Christmas. When you've determined the elements you want in your show, form groups to begin piecing the parts together. For example, you'll need a couple of groups to go out and take slide pictures or video footage of the items they're including in the show.

Help group members piece the elements together into a cohesive show that includes lots of sights and sounds. For example, a show might begin with a picture of Santa and recorded interviews with little children about what Christmas means to them, then lead into a slide show or skit about the true meaning of Christmas or to a song such as "Silent Night."

When the project is complete, have kids present it to the whole church. Afterward, have kids explain how they felt as the project unfolded and as the finished program was shown to the church.

Scriptures for Deeper Study: Matthew 1:21; Acts 16:31.

Snow Nativity
(Advent, December)

Focus of the Fun: Kids will create a snow sculpture depicting a nativity scene.

Supplies: Snow, children's books on Jesus' birth, hot chocolate, and Bibles.

For this project, you'll need lots of wet, snowball-quality snow.

When the conditions are right, call kids to your church to create a nativity scene entirely out of snow. A good place for this scene is in front of your church.

Young-Teenager Tip:
Les Christie, youth worker, speaker, and author, says, "It's unrealistic to expect young adolescents to sit in a chair for an hour-and-a-half lecture." Christie suggests that junior high workers "use 10- or 15-minute segments with junior highers and keep them moving and doing things." (Les Christie, "16 Ways You Can Earn Your Kids' Respect," JR. HIGH MINISTRY Magazine)

Have kids refer to the first chapters of Luke and to children's books on the birth of Christ for ideas on what to include in the nativity.

To involve everyone in the project, assign a different part of the scene to each group of two or three people. For example, one group might work on the manger while another works on Mary or Joseph. Allow kids the freedom to create a realistic or an abstract version of the nativity. Let them decide.

When the project is complete, enjoy hot chocolate and form groups of no more than four. Have kids discuss the following questions: **What was it like to spend so much time out in the cold? How is that like the way Mary and Joseph might have felt when they couldn't find a room at an inn and had to stay in the barn? What is significant about Jesus' humble birth? Why did God choose to send Jesus to be born as a baby?**

Scripture for Deeper Study: Matthew 1:18—2:12.

World's Largest Christmas Card
(Advent, December)

Focus of the Fun: Junior highers and middle schoolers will use sheets of drywall to construct a huge Christmas card for all church members to enjoy at church.

Supplies: Two sheets of drywall, duct tape, permanent markers, Christmas cards, and Bibles.

Before the Christmas season, have kids meet to create a huge Christmas card. You'll need two sheets of drywall and a roll of duct tape to build the card. Have kids help you assemble the two sheets of drywall by taping them together, using the tape as a hinge. Be sure you have plenty of space where you're working on the project to lay the card on the floor, then stand it up when you're done.

After creating the card, have kids decorate it with large permanent markers. Have a number of Christmas cards available for kids to look at and get ideas for the giant card. They may want to use one of the designs from the regular-size cards.

Inside the card have kids write a message to the whole church wishing them a joyful Christmas. Leave a space on the back (where the card company logo usually is) for kids to sign their names. When the card is complete, have kids move it into the foyer of your church to surprise church-goers.

When the card is in place, have kids meet near it for a brief discussion. Ask: **What was it like to create this big card for our church? How is the size of this card like the "bigness" of God's gift to us in Jesus?** Have someone close the project time by reading aloud Matthew 1:23.

Scriptures for Deeper Study: Isaiah 9:6-7; Micah 5:2-5; Matthew 1:18-2:12; Luke 2; Acts 16:31.

New Year's Eve Countdown (December 31)

Focus of the Fun: Kids will create a device for counting down the last hour to the new year and discuss waiting for Jesus to return.

Supplies: One sheet of newsprint, masking tape, markers, and Bibles. The rest of the supplies will be decided by the group.

Use this project to create a mechanism for counting down the last hour to the new year and to illustrate the idea of waiting for Jesus Christ's return.

On the afternoon before New Year's Day, have your students meet at a place where you will have a New Year's Eve party. Say: **We are going to create and construct a way to count down the last 60 minutes of this year.** Have your group brainstorm a countdown device they can create, or use one of these ideas.

● Inflate 60 balloons and tape them to a wall in a line leading toward a new-year sign. Pop one balloon each minute of the last hour.

● Create a marble maze with toilet paper rolls and paper towel rolls. Fill a jar with 60 marbles, then have kids roll a marble from the jar through the maze each minute until midnight.

While kids brainstorm, write their ideas on newsprint . After the brainstorming, have kids choose one idea to implement. Then gather the materials and create the device.

At 11 p.m. on New Year's Eve, start the countdown. Then gather your group for a discussion. During the discussion, allow kids to get up every minute to do the countdown procedure. Make sure that every student has a chance to participate in the countdown. Ask: **How do you feel while we are counting down the minutes to the new year? What do you anticipate for the new year?**

Have the group read Matthew 24:36-51 aloud, with each student reading one verse until the group has read the whole passage. If you have more students than verses, form pairs and have each pair read one verse aloud in unison. Ask: **What does this passage say about how we need to look forward to Christ's return? What does that mean for us on a daily basis? What is one thing you can do in the new year to help you anticipate Christ's return?**

Scriptures for Deeper Study: Proverbs 27:1; John 6:40; 1 Corinthians 15:51-52; 2 Peter 3:8-10.

The Any-Holiday Anticipation Calendar

Focus of the Fun: Kids will create calendars to count down the days to a special event and discuss the need for patience.

Supplies: Scrap paper, pencils, newsprint, 20×30-inch construction paper, cookie cutters, masking tape, markers, scissors, stickers, rubber stamps and ink pads, and Bibles.

U se this project to help kids explore the idea of patience.

This project borrows from the Advent-calendar tradition used to count the days until Christmas. The anticipation calendar can be used to count the days toward any holiday or any other fun day, such as a birthday, graduation, or a group activity.

Say: **We are going to create anticipation calendars for one another. These calendars will help us look forward to a fun day in the future.**

Have each student write his or her name on a piece of paper, fold the paper, and hand it back to you. Fan out the pieces of paper in your hands and allow each student to pick one. Make sure that each student chooses someone else's name.

Give each student one piece of newsprint and one piece of construction paper. On the construction paper, have kids create at least 10 "doors" by tracing around a variety of cookie cutters to create different shapes, or have them draw their own shapes. Instruct kids to cut out the doors, leaving a little bit of a hinge attached to the paper. Then have kids place the construction paper over the newsprint and trace the outline of each door onto the newsprint. Have kids remove the construction paper and create pictures or encouraging sayings within the outlined spaces on the newsprint. Have them create the pictures using markers, stickers, rubber stamps and ink pads, or any other creative way they want.

When the students have finished all of their pictures, have them tape the construction paper to the newsprint so each door corresponds with the appropri-

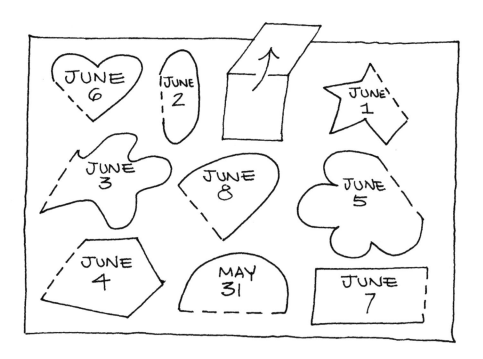

ate space on the newsprint. Then have them label each door with a date that counts down to the big event. For example, if the anticipation calendar is for graduation on June 8, the students would label their doors from May 30 until June 8. Have students give their completed calendars to the person whose name they chose at the beginning of the meeting, and instruct each person to open the calendar doors on the days written on them.

Ask: **What is it like to wait for something you are looking forward to? What do you do to help you wait? What do you think it will be like to use our anticipation calendars when waiting for a big event? In what other situations do we need patience?**

Form two groups. Have groups alternate reading aloud the verses in James 5:7-11. Ask: **What does this passage say about patience? What is one thing we can do to become more patient?**

Young-Teenager Tip: Enjoy the time you have now with your young teenagers. Before you know it they'll be on their own, building their own families . . . they'll be older. Which means that you'll be old . . . er, too. Kinda makes you want to keep those kids forever, doesn't it?

Scriptures for Deeper Study: Matthew 6:34; Romans 2:7; Galatians 5:22-23; Ephesians 4:2.

Birthday Surprises

Focus of the Fun: Junior highers and middle schoolers will brainstorm a dozen or more different ways to surprise people on their birthdays, then use those ideas to celebrate group members' birthdays.

Supplies: Variety of supplies as determined by group members.

When kids get tired of the same old birthday celebrations, have them brainstorm a dozen or more new ones. Form groups of no more than five. Have each group read Romans 12:15 and think of inexpensive and fun ways to make group members' birthdays an occasion for group rejoicing. Here are a few ideas to get kids thinking.

● Kids could take the birthday person out for a free game of bowling.

● Kids could give the birthday person a gift of a food item from their home.

● Kids could carry the person around on a chair "throne" during the meeting closest to his or her birthday.

● Kids could all call the person on his or her birthday to sing "Happy Birthday."

Encourage both serious and wild ideas, then choose a dozen or so that are easily done. Write each on a separate slip of paper and place them in a box. Then, each time you want to celebrate someone's birthday, have a volunteer choose a paper slip to determine what the kids will do. When you've exhausted all the ideas, have another brainstorming time. Be sure to get lots of ideas from the people whose birthdays were celebrated with the previous ideas.

Young-Teenager Tip: When your kids are feeling down because they think they're too young to make a difference, remind them of the impact David had on one giant named Goliath. Or let them know that Jeremiah, a famous prophet, was all of 19 or 20 when he began his ministry. Sometimes young teenagers need to be reminded that they *do* matter and can make a difference.

Scriptures for Deeper Study: Luke 15:22-24; Nahum 1:15.

National Rainbow Day (You pick the date for this one!)

Focus of the Fun: Kids will create rainbows and discuss God's promises.

Supplies: One Bible for every four students. The rest of the supplies will be determined by the students.

Have kids form groups of no more than four. Say: **Each group is going to create a rainbow in a new, creative way. You can use any materials, but you cannot color or paint a rainbow onto a piece of paper. Use your imagination to create a rainbow in an unusual way.** Set a deadline for the group to meet in three hours in your youth room with their rainbows.

If your students are struggling for ideas, you may wish to suggest one or more of these ideas:

● tacking red, orange, yellow, green, blue, and purple strips of crepe paper to the ceiling of the youth room;

- creating a cooking-oil slick in a bowl by filling the bowl half with water and half with cooking oil and shining a flashlight on it to find the rainbow;
- baking a yellow cake, frosting it with white icing, and covering it with rows of Skittles; or
- dressing in rainbow-colored clothing—one person wears red, another wears an orange top and yellow pants, another wears a green top and blue pants, and a fourth wears purple. Then this group lays on the ground to form a rainbow-colored line.

When the group has gathered, have each foursome share their rainbow. Then have each foursome read Genesis 9:8-17, with each group member reading two or three verses aloud. Have each group brainstorm one sentence that summarizes the passage. Then have groups share their sentences with the larger group. Say: **God made a promise to Noah. What other promises has he made to us? How do we know that God will keep his promises? What is one promise God has made that he has kept for you?**

Scriptures for Deeper Study: Joshua 23:14; Romans 15:8; Hebrews 6:13-20.

Young-Teenager Tip: You can't get water from a well that has run dry. Remember to rejuvenate yourself by spending your own time with God. Also create a list of five things that you find relaxing—reading a good book, baking, or playing volleyball—and schedule time weekly to do at least one of those things.

Party Time

Focus of the Fun: Group members will prepare confetti to celebrate special holiday events in the church.

Supplies: Variety of wrapping paper and scrap paper, scissors, plastic bags, and Bibles.

Have kids invite congregation members to donate their scrap pieces of wrapping paper to the youth group. Then have kids collect other scrap paper and meet for a "confetti-tearing" party. During the project, have kids enjoy being together while they tear and cut the paper into tiny bits of confetti for use in church celebrations.

Make the confetti party more interesting by having kids determine which colors of confetti are appropriate for each of the following events: birthdays, Easter, Independence Day, Christmas, and New Year's Day. Then have kids arrange their confetti pieces into these colors and put them into plastic bags for later use during those events. Save one or two bags of confetti to celebrate the end of the confetti party.

While junior highers and middle schoolers are working on their confetti, read aloud Luke 15:22-24 and have kids tell about when they've felt most "celebrated" in life. At the end of the party, have kids stand in a circle. One at a time, have kids toss a little confetti onto the person on their right and tell one reason that person is worth celebrating. Then have kids toss the rest of the confetti at the same time while shouting, "Being a Christian is something to celebrate!"

Use the confetti kids have created throughout the year to celebrate events in the youth group or in the whole church. Just remember that for every tossed confetti, there is an equal and opposite force called "cleanup."

Scripture for Deeper Study: Nahum 1:15.

Transitional Parties

Focus of the Fun: Kids will coordinate parties that celebrate the changing seasons.

Supplies: Seasonal decorations and foods, and Bibles.

To celebrate the changing seasons, have junior highers and middle schoolers plan and enjoy parties with seasonal themes that change midway through the party. For example, kids might decorate one room with summer decorations and plan foods such as watermelon and iced tea, and decorate another room with fall items and plan foods such as pumpkin pie and turkey.

Each time the seasons change, have kids prepare and enjoy a transitional party. During the parties, have kids reminisce about the events of the past season and think about the upcoming season's activities. Have kids read Ecclesiastes 3:1-8 and discuss what it's like to experience change in life. Ask: **What are the most difficult changes to adjust to? What are good ways for dealing with change? What emotions are you experiencing with this changing season? How are the feelings we have during the changing seasons like the feelings we have when we face other changes?**

Junior highers and middle schoolers may enjoy planning and putting on a transitional party for their parents or for younger children, too.

Young-Teenager Tip:
If the projects in this book have inspired you, and you want to develop your own innovative project ideas for young teenagers, consider checking out Roger von Oech's *Creative Whack Pack* (published by U.S. Games Systems, Inc.). The *Creative Whack Pack* is a deck of 64 cards with methods to help you think creatively while developing your own new, never-been-done-before ideas.

Scriptures for Deeper Study: James 1:17-18; Malachi 3:6a.

Evaluation of Fun Bible-Learning Projects for Young Teenagers

Please help Group Publishing, Inc. continue providing innovative and useable resources for youth ministry by taking a moment to fill out and send us this evaluation. Thanks!

• • •

1. As a whole, this book has been (circle one):

Not much help   Very Helpful

1   2   3   4   5   6   7   8   9   10

2. The things I liked best about this book were:

3. This book could be improved by:

4. One thing I'll do differently because of this book is:

5. Optional Information:

Name _____

Street Address _____

City_____ State _____Zip _____

Phone Number _____ Date _____

Tackle important issues in the lives of your teenagers with **Active Bible Curriculum**®. Help your teenagers learn the Bible and discover how to apply it to their daily lives. And save your church money—each book includes a complete teachers guide, handout masters you can photocopy, publicity helps, and bonus ideas—all for one low price.

FOR JUNIOR HIGH/MIDDLE SCHOOL:

Accepting Others: Beyond Barriers & Stereotypes, ISBN 1-55945-126-2

Advice to Young Christians: Exploring Paul's Letters, ISBN 1-55945-146-7

Applying the Bible to Life, ISBN 1-55945-116-5

Becoming Responsible, ISBN 1-55945-109-2

Bible Heroes: Joseph, Esther, Mary & Peter ISBN 1-55945-137-8

Boosting Self-Esteem, ISBN 1-55945-100-9

Building Better Friendships, ISBN 1-55945-138-6

Can Christians Have Fun?, ISBN 1-55945-134-3

Christmas: A Fresh Look, ISBN 1-55945-124-6

Dealing With Disappointment, ISBN 1-55945-139-4

Doing Your Best, ISBN 1-55945-142-4

Evil and the Occult, ISBN 1-55945-102-5

Guys & Girls: Understanding Each Other, ISBN 1-55945-110-6

Handling Conflict, ISBN 1-55945-125-4

Is God Unfair?, ISBN 1-55945-108-4

Peer Pressure, ISBN 1-55945-103-3

Prayer, ISBN 1-55945-104-1

Telling Your Friends About Christ, ISBN 1-55945-114-9

The Ten Commandments, ISBN 1-55945-127-0

Today's Media: Choosing Wisely, ISBN 1-55945-144-0

Today's Music: Good or Bad?, ISBN 1-55945-101-7

What Is God's Purpose for Me?, ISBN 1-55945-132-7

What's a Christian?, ISBN 1-55945-105-X

...and many more!

FOR SENIOR HIGH:

1 & 2 Corinthians: Christian Discipleship, ISBN 1-55945-230-7

Angels, Demons, Miracles & Prayer, ISBN 1-55945-235-8

Changing the World, ISBN 1-55945-236-6

Christians in a Non-Christian World, ISBN 1-55945-224-2

Counterfeit Religions, ISBN 1-55945-207-2

Dating Decisions, ISBN 1-55945-215-3

Dealing With Life's Pressures, ISBN 1-55945-232-3

Deciphering Jesus' Parables, ISBN 1-55945-237-4

Exploring Ethical Issues, ISBN 1-55945-225-0

Faith for Tough Times, ISBN 1-55945-216-1

Getting Along With Parents, ISBN 1-55945-202-1

The Gospel of John: Jesus' Teachings, ISBN 1-55945-208-0

Hazardous to Your Health: AIDS, Steroids & Eating Disorders, ISBN 1-55945-200-5

Is Marriage in Your Future?, ISBN 1-55945-203-X

Knowing God's Will, ISBN 1-55945-205-6

Making Good Decisions, ISBN 1-55945-209-9

Movies, Music, TV & Me, ISBN 1-55945-213-7

Real People, Real Faith, ISBN 1-55945-238-2

Revelation, ISBN 1-55945-229-3

School Struggles, ISBN 1-55945-201-3

Sex: A Christian Perspective, ISBN 1-55945-206-4

Who Is God?, ISBN 1-55945-218-8

Who Is Jesus?, ISBN 1-55945-219-6

Who Is the Holy Spirit?, ISBN 1-55945-217-X

Your Life as a Disciple, ISBN 1-55945-204-8

...and many more!

PUT FAITH INTO ACTION...

...with Group's **Projects With a Purpose**™ **for Youth Ministry.**

Want to try something different with your 7th-12th grade classes? Group's **Projects With a Purpose**™ **for Youth Ministry** offers four-week courses that really get kids into their faith. Each **Project With a Purpose** course gives you tools to facilitate a project that will provide a direct, purposeful learning experience. Teenagers will discover something significant about their faith while learning the importance of working together, sharing one another's troubles, and supporting one another in love...plus they'll have lots of fun! For Sunday school classes, midweek meetings, home Bible studies, youth groups, retreats, or any time you want to help teenagers discover more about their faith.

Acting Out Jesus' Parables
Strengthen your teenagers' faith as they are challenged to understand the parables' descriptions of the Christian life. Explore such key issues as the value of humility and the importance of hope.   ISBN 1-55945-147-5

Celebrating Christ With Youth-Led Worship
Kids love to celebrate. For Christians, Jesus is the ultimate reason to celebrate. And as kids celebrate Jesus, they'll grow closer to him—an excitement that will be shared with the whole congregation.   ISBN 1-55945-410-5

Checking Your Church's Pulse
Your teenagers will find new meaning for their faith with this course. Interviews with congregational members will help your teenagers, and your church, grow closer together.   ISBN 1-55945-408-3

Serving Your Neighbors
Strengthen the "service heart" in your teenagers. They'll appreciate the importance of serving others as they follow Jesus' example.   ISBN 1-55945-406-7

Sharing Your Faith Without Fear
Teenagers don't have to be great orators to share with others what God's love means to them. Teach them to express their faith through everyday actions without fear of rejection.   ISBN 1-55945-409-1

Teaching Teenagers to Pray
Watch as your teenagers develop strong, effective prayer lives as you introduce them to the basics of prayer. They'll learn how to pray with and for others.   ISBN 1-55945-407-5

Teenagers Teaching Children
Teach your teenagers how to share the Gospel with children. Through this course, your teenagers will learn more about their faith by teaching others and develop teaching skills to last a lifetime.   ISBN 1-55945-405-9

Videotaping Your Church Members' Faith Stories
Teenagers will enjoy learning about their congregation members with this exciting video project. And, they'll learn the depth and power of God's faithfulness to his people.   ISBN 1-55945-239-0

Order today from your local Christian bookstore, or write: Group Publishing, Box 485, Loveland, CO 80539.

MORE INNOVATIVE RESOURCES
FOR YOUR MINISTRY

The Youth Worker's Encyclopedia of Bible-Teaching Ideas:
Old Testament/ New Testament

Explore the most comprehensive idea-books available for youth workers! Discover more than 350 creative ideas in each of these 400-page encyclopedias—there's at least one idea for each and every book of the Bible. Find ideas for...retreats and overnighters, learning games, adventures, special projects, parties, prayers, music, devotions, skits, and much more!

Plus, you can use these ideas for groups of all sizes in any setting. Large or small. Sunday or mid-week meeting. Bible study. Sunday school class or retreat. Discover exciting new ways to teach each book of the Bible to your youth group.

Old Testament   ISBN 1-55945-184-X
New Testament   ISBN 1-55945-183-1

Clip-Art Cartoons for Churches

Here are over 180 funny, photocopiable illustrations to help you jazz up your calendars, newsletters, posters, fliers, transparencies, postcards, business cards, announcements—all your printed materials! These fun, fresh illustrations cover a variety of church and Christian themes, including church life, Sunday school, youth groups, school life, sermons, church events, volunteers, and more! And there's a variety of artistic styles to choose from so each piece you create will be unique and original.

Each illustration is provided in different sizes so it's easy to use. You won't find random images here...each image is a complete cartoon. And these cartoons are fun! In fact, they're so entertaining that you may just find yourself reading the book and not photocopying them at all.

Order your copy of **Clip-Art Cartoons for Churches** today...and add some spice to your next printed piece.

ISBN 1-55945-791-0

Bore No More! (For Every Pastor, Speaker, Teacher)

This book is a must for every pastor, youth leader, teacher, and speaker. These 70 audience-grabbing activities pull listeners into your lesson or sermon—and drive your message home!

Discover clever object lessons, creative skits, and readings. Music and celebration ideas. Affirmation activities. All the innovative techniques 85 percent of adult churchgoers say they wish their pastors would try! (recent Group Publishing poll)

Involve your congregation in the learning process! These complete 5- to 15-minute activities highlight common New Testament Lectionary passages, so you'll use this book week after week.

ISBN 1-55945-266-8

Order today from your local Christian bookstore, or write:
Group Publishing, Box 485, Loveland, CO 80539.